The Anatomy of Financial Success

The Key to Building Financial Confidence and Destroying Your Insecurities About Money

Elijah Bilel

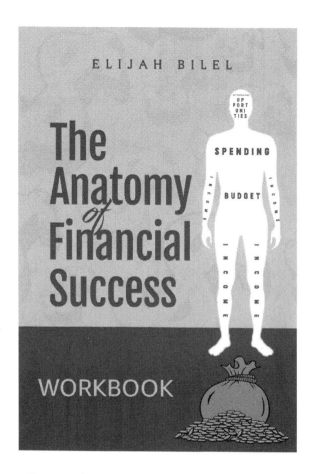

Download your free workbook

Read this first

Just as a thank you for getting my book, you can receive the workbook for the book free!

The Anatomy of Financial Success Workbook is the perfect companion to The Anatomy of Financial Success Book. This workbook will help you take and implement the knowledge and ideas from the book and apply them to your life relating to finances.

Click here to download

(Or go to www.financialanatomy.net/bookresources)

CONTENTS

INTRODUCTION

We all have different financial wants, desires and needs. The mystery of life in the financial world is finding a method to fulfill those in a way that we can both enjoy and appreciate. The only problem is that we don't have the right tools. This hardly seems fair, right? Even when trying to solve a puzzle, you are at least given all of the puzzle pieces. You see what piece fits where and make appropriate adjustments from there. Sad to say that it's not the case in the financial world. You are just thrust in it and expected to succeed.

When it's put like that, it seems like a cruel and random world. Is this what the financial world is like? Of course, not! There is more to it than that. What if I told you that this financial world actually has puzzle pieces that you can put together. The only difference between a puzzle piece on a board game and this one is that you can't see the parts without the right mindset. A piece could be staring you in the face, but you don't see it. After stumbling through the world making mistakes, you finally start seeing the pieces. Finally, my financial problems are solved! Right? Nope, it's just the beginning.

Through trial and error, you finally see the pieces. How the heck do the pieces go together in the puzzle? More importantly, what is the puzzle constructing? In a board game puzzle, when you finally finish the puzzle, it reveals the image that the pieces make. What are the pieces creating in this financial world of ours? The image that the pieces form is your own financial person. That person will be different for all of us based on what we want, need, and desire financially. Sadly, most people will never be able to put together their financial person entirely because they lack both the blueprint and the know-how on how to put it together. That is what this book is written to address. Anytime you are not happy with your financial life, it is because of one of the following 4 reasons:

1. You can't or don't know how to increase your income in the way you want to.

2. Your money goes in and out of your bank accounts. In other words, you don't know how to budget your money.

3. Spending or not spending money on certain things stress you out.

4. You don't know how you want to make money.

Do you know what all these things have in common? They all stem from a lack of control over your earnings vs. spending ratio. You will find that all financial problems branch off one or more of these deficiencies. Many people try to ignore these and pretend that they will go away. That is like not sewing the hole in your pocket while it keeps getting bigger and bigger until your wallet finally falls through it. The answer to these questions is foundational to any person who is thriving financially. Without the answers to them, a person cannot help but be financially insecure. These are legitimate and real problems, and no one answer will serve us all. Do we all want and need the same thing financial? Obviously not and that is why this book is so important. So, you can construct your financial person and solve not just one but all of these 4 problems that at some point, you have or will come across.

Financial Self-Confidence

One day, I had an enlightening experience. It was back in the days when I drove for Ubereats to make extra money. Things were tight, and it required me to be somewhat thrifty. I was working on some things on the side that would produce income in the future but none presently. I knew this and had no problem with it, but it didn't change the fact that it would be a bumpy ride until they took off.

I went to visit my mom, and while I was there, she told me about how her refrigerator had gone out. Even though my money was tight, I wasn't going to have my mom in her house with no refrigerator. I gave her one of my debit cards and told her to go and make arrangements to have another refrigerator delivered. She could put the down payment on my card. Later that week around 8.30 pm, I was in the middle of a delivery for Ubereats when it started pouring down rain. Ironically, I was listening to the music on my iPod when the song by DMX "The Rain" started playing. I'm not by any means endorsing the lyrics, but what's important here was the chorus *"Only I can stop the rain."* It was at that moment that I realized the real benefit of having my financial person put together.

Calling it quits and going home wouldn't have been the best thing since I had financial obligations to meet. This situation was not the lowest I've been, as I have had more stringent scenarios financially before. It occurred to me just at this moment that money had lost the ability to affect me negatively on any significant level. I knew what I wanted, and I knew what it took to get there. I was entirely at peace with it. The struggles that I was going through were simply part of the process. This is what I want for every one of you. That liberating feeling of knowing what you want and what it brings in its entirety, both positive and negative. We love to focus on the positive things of what we want, but there are unfavorable sides too. It comes down to if you value what you want enough and if you're willing to put up with what you don't want. This opens the door for you to be fully satisfied with what you aim to achieve financially and not to be disappointed with what comes along with having it.

It is my desire that you set the most ambitious goals you can and have the tools you need to achieve them. As you proceed throughout the book, you will grow the financial skin you need, develop the guns you need to increase your income, strengthen the core you need to budget any money that comes your way, work out the financial pecs you need to spend money with confidence, and develop the x-ray vision you need to evaluate financial opportunities that you seek out or that come your way. It is this information and system that I'm sharing in this book that built The App Lifestyle and manages the money generated from it. If you are sincere about learning, I promise that you will be a different person by the time you finish this book. This will come from building your financial person so that you can navigate through this financial world, and it can, in turn, bring you all the things you desire financially. Don't delay or your financial visions will quickly turn into dreams. Feeling like they are outside the scope of you achieving them. Let's get started on building your financial person RIGHT NOW!

This book is broken up into 5 phases. Each phase is in itself a system that can be used to clean up or build that particular area of your financial person. Like the human body, each system is part of a greater whole. Based on your personality and experiences, you will find that you will be firm in some areas, and others will need more work. The chapters in each phase have assignments that are designed to develop that area of that phase. Completing the assignments is the key if you want the maximum benefits of this book. Learning and mastering this book is essential in building your financial person.

Phase 1: What is money? Without realizing it, we often pick up fallacies about money, like "money is the root of all evil," or doing certain things for money is wrong. The judgment of money is simple. What are the answers to these 3 questions? Is what I'm doing hurting someone? Is what I'm doing helping someone? Is what I'm doing helping myself or my family? If you can answer "no, yes and yes," respectively, then you're good to go. After reading this phase, you will have grown the financial skin you need to repeal such erroneous assumptions about money that subtly sabotage your attempts at acquiring it. Your financial skin is that layer that protects and repeals harmful and limiting beliefs about money that hold a person back from reaching their full potential.

Phase 2 (Income): Why does money have the effect it has on us? Does it have the ability to make us happy, sad, angry, depressed, etc.? We often desire more money, whether it be based on our wants and/or needs. Have you ever stopped to wonder what the answer would be if you asked anyone on the streets if he or she wanted to be wealthy? Most would shout "Yes!" But, if you ask them "How," you will most likely hear cricket sounds.

In the same way that a doctor cannot operate on a human body without the knowledge of the anatomy of the body, one cannot build wealth without the understanding of how income is built. In this phase, you will learn the different types of income, how they differ, and which one(s) are best for you based on what you want. This phase will develop your financial arms and legs so that they are strong enough to take you anywhere financially you want to go.

Phase 3 (Budgeting): A budget is unique to everyone. With that being said, there are things that will always remain fundamental to a successful budget. The definition of a successful budget is one that is always moving you forward financially in life. Without this, people stagnate or even move backward. How do you prevent this? How do you not only stay on track with your goals but ensure that your progress financially isn't immediately undone by some unplanned event? At the end of this phase, you will have the blueprint to ensure you are always moving forward. This phase will develop your financial core so that you can stomach any increase or decrease in income and still make progress towards your goals.

Phase 4 (Spending): Ever wonder why money is such a diverse subject? Why can you take 3 people and have them spend money on the exact same thing, and all 3 of them can experience different emotions? It is this that is the foundation of why some of us are good at certain things when it comes to money, and some of us are not. We ALL have strengths and weaknesses we need to work on when it comes to this subject. When you spend money on something, do you ever feel anxious, guilty or uneasy? Maybe sometimes all of the above.

On the flip side, I'm sure we've spent money and felt empowered, happy, and great. What produces that feeling? If we want to get further into it, you'll find that some things you automatically spend money on and others you feel the said emotions with a piece of hesitation. This is because of a lack of perspective. How do we identify our strengths and build off them? How can we identify our weaknesses and address them? The ultimate question is, how does one go about changing their perspective so that they don't feel this way? By the end of this phase, you will be able to answer that question and actively do something about it, giving you a renewed sense of confidence. This phase will develop your financial chest and make them bulky; giving you the confidence you need financially to trust yourself. This phase will also establish your financial back or backbone, so you have a spine to acknowledge your weaknesses in spending so that you can do something about them.

Phase 5 (Evaluating opportunities): Opportunities are presented to us sometimes literally daily. You should get this job. You should start your own business. You should make money online. You should join this network marketing company. You should write a book. These are just a few examples. Ideas like this are being shot your way either by others, or by yourself (mentally). How do you evaluate what a good financial opportunity for you is? What are the criteria for an excellent opportunity? Not knowing this information can be stressful within itself. The worst-case scenario is if you don't take advantage of your chance and your mind keeps screaming "What if" scenarios. Even worse, you accept the opportunity only to find out that it's not working out and you end up walking away. Sounds like a drag, right? After this phase, you will have the ability to take any opportunity presented to you and evaluate it within a few minutes to determine whether it is a sweet opportunity for you and if it can bring you closer to your goals. This phase will develop your financial head and eyes which will give you financial x-ray vision to see the inner workings of an opportunity and see if it is right for you.

Are you ready to build your financial person? Let's get the ball rolling starting with Phase 1!

The History of Our Financial World

For us to understand where we are now, we have to look at how we got here. This requires us to take a look at the history that lead us to where we are today. Where are we today? We are in a world where many struggle financially. Not because of solely not having enough money, but because we lack the education and perspective about cash, which in turn, makes us financially insecure. This insecurity has a way of bleeding over into the other big areas of life, such as career, relationships, and friendships, to name a few. Was it always like this,

11

though? As Dr. Lanning's hologram in the movie I, Robot said to Will Smith throughout the movie, "That detective, is the right question."

The subject of money is something that we can all relate to, whether we want to or not. It is something we deal with in our everyday lives and is connected to both our wants and needs in today's society. Have you ever stopped to wonder why is it that we learn so little about it in school? School is meant to prepare us for the real world, right? Regardless of your chosen profession, you are going to need what I refer to in this book as financial savviness, if you want to be successful in the real world. Why is it that something as universal as money is not covered in school? The answer is two words. Indentured servitude! It isn't directly implied, but rather the result that occurs from not having financial savviness. One must have a balance of these two things when it comes to money.

1. How much income they generate?

2. How much money they spend to achieve what they want in life?

3. Without a balance of these 2, you end up putting yourself in a financial quagmire.

4. You spend more than you make, or you don't make enough money. To understand where we have ended up though, we have to see where we have been.

How Did We End Up Here?

In the 1800s, the school system in America as we know it was very different. They used a method of teaching known as the monitoring system. Teachers would select students with the highest exam scores and promote them to what they call monitors. These monitors were responsible for teaching the other students themselves. The actual teacher of the class played more of an overseer role. They learned the basics of reading, writing, arithmetic, history, grammar, rhetoric, and geography. To many people's surprise, the duration of school, in general, was only up to the 8th grade. After this point, children traditionally learned the trade of their family.

Along with this was how their family handled finances within their profession. This means the primary way that people learned about money, and its secrets, were through direct mentorship from their parent or parent-like figure. At this time, people mainly made their money by leveraging a trade and building a mom and pop operation around it. To keep this type of business afloat, a person had to learn pretty quickly how to balance their earnings rate with their consumption rate. Their children would subtly pick up on how to do this, so when it was their turn, they were well equipped to handle the real world. The degree to which a person could do this was a direct indication of how successful they would be financially. That is still the case today. The only difference is that most people actively knew this and respected it.

This had many subtle but impactful effects on how they learned about money. It was a mentor and apprentice scenario. The mentor often would have the apprentice actively engage in the tasks that they would do. For example, the mentor may have had his/her apprentice do part of the accounting for that day's work. The mentor would have the apprentice measure the margins between each product sold and how much profit was made. These types of tasks gave the apprentice direct experience with money, and many times worked their ability to think on their feet. The ability to think on your feet when it comes to $$$ is the epitome of financial savviness. It gets their emotions involved and gets them to use the information that they have learned to get the desired result they want. That aforementioned statement may have summed up the primary skill of life in general.

Little did everyone know that changes were coming. Over the years, the focus of education shifted from mostly being the family's responsibility to being the job of the government. When this happened, the learning of being financially savvy with your money was no longer the go-to method of teaching your child. At the same time, the government didn't find it was in their best interest to incorporate a financial curriculum into the school system. The government needed a way to make money from its citizens directly. This would typically be in form of taxes, but the nation was founded off of the concept of not getting taxed. It would be far too soon to monazite the citizens like this. It would be too "British," and citizens would respond hastily to that. Instead, financial education or financial savviness, as I like to call it, was omitted from school. The only time it was available was in college, which required payment, and only if your major was something in the finance sector like business or accounting. Does that sound familiar?

Without the financial savviness of keeping one's earning rate and consumption rate in check, it was inevitable that people started to get in debt one way or another. This could be taking on debt to get things you want or need, but without the critical thinking required to see if that would be the best thing for you in that instance. At the same time, the financial IQ of the average person started to drop since they did not have the vision to see things for what they are. This laid the groundwork for the government to slowly start introducing taxes that before would have been revolted against. Every few years, taxes would go up, or new ones would get added, and the public would get pissed for a while and then shrug it off. Yes, they were upset, but it was coming from the simple fact of just paying more money, and not from the realization that it was against their core principles. With their financial savviness dropping further and further, taxes kept rising more and more. Since the people lacked the financial savviness, the average debt a person took on kept increasing. Retailers, merchants, businesses, and institutions were taxed more, so this indirectly allowed the government to do what they initially wanted, which was to monetize their citizens. Eventually, they could start doing this directly in the form of sales tax.

That is how we have arrived where we are today. Instead of money being taught in high school and required as basics in college, it is omitted from high school and limited in college. Basics in college are simply a rehash of what was taught in high school only with slightly more detail. If you don't agree with me, take a good look at how the basics someone takes in college directly affects their success in life? Even those outside of the U.S. are being indirectly affected since many developing and developed countries are attempting to mimic the blueprint popularized by America. So, what is the solution for both ourselves and society as a whole? We have to bring financial savviness back. It is the lack of it that plagues our current civilization; government included (e.g., U.S. national debt is over $22 trillion as of this writing). It is the science behind us obtaining what we financially want without the means coming back to haunt us in some way. We have to learn both the fundamentals of money and how they fit in our modern-day society. If the school system won't teach us and our immediate family knows little about how to be financially savvy, what do we do? Herein lies the need for this book.

We've used the phrase "financial savviness" a lot in this Introduction. What does it mean though? The dictionary defines savviness as "shrewdness and practical knowledge; the ability to make good judgments." The word financial is defined as "relating to finance." Putting them together is the ability to make good judgments based on practical knowledge when it comes to finances. While those are the dictionary equivalents, I'd like to take it a step further and say it's "the science of managing your finances that keeps you moving forward financially."

The thing about learning is the results are often amplified when you have a partner. We also have to admit that it's more fun too, right? That's why I highly recommend that you go threw this adventure with another person. Your friend, sister, brother, acquaintance, or significant other. Do you think you have a monopoly on financial problems? Guess again! We all know someone who either feels they're not living up to their full financial potential or that is struggling in one or more of the main areas of personal finance. You see, every person needs to know the following:

1. How to increase and identify different types of income

2. How to budget, both your money and your emotions

3. How to spend money in a way that it never sets you back

4. How to evaluate money-making opportunities as they come your way

It is the capability to do these 4 things that make a strong financial person. With that statement being made, this question is probably coming to mind. Since it is so important to learn this, though, how do we go about learning how to be a strong financial person?

PHASE 1.

CHAPTER 1.

HOW WE LEARN AS HUMANS

Things may change in society, but one thing that will always stay the same is how humans learn, interpret, and adapt. When it comes to learning anything new about a subject, you have to look at what has been out there on it for years. Money is no exception. Yet, it would be incredibly redundant to list everything people and society deem is right and wrong about money. This chapter would be as long as a dictionary. Instead, we have to look at the underlining theme that ensures success in learning and applying anything. In doing so, we see how those factors are missing in our own views of money and finances. Only then can we know how these missing factors are inhibiting success in the said subject. The subject, in this case, being money and finances. To effectively use something, you have to learn it, and anything that you use to assist yourself in the learning of it is critical to long-term retention. That means we must put an enthuses on learning itself.

There are many styles of learning, and society has many ways of measuring the effectiveness of these styles. The most successful forms of learning always have the following in common:

1. It is done in such a way that the person sees a direct correlation to a goal.

2. It is fun for the participant.

The 1st factor has an obvious implication. It is often overlooked, yet it is the reason for wanting to learn the information or skill in the first place. The 2nd one acts as the passion that gives fuel to the goal. It is simply human nature to expect something in exchange for doing some type of work, for when an expectation (in this case, a goal) is not in mind, the person will become disinterested or bored. If you want an example of this, look at how the education system is set up in America. Except for college, most children have no real goal that they are emotionally attached to. For those that do, there is often not a focus on how the information being taught to them fits in their game plan to reach this goal.

Take for instance, a 3rd grader named Jeff who wants to be a firefighter. Jeff's class has no interest in the math being taught. To them, it is the equivalent of watching wallpaper dry. They just find it so dull. Luckily for them, they have an awesome teacher named Mr. Smith. One day after the school bell had just rung, signaling that the school day was officially over, Mr. Smith saw Jeff slowly packing up his backpack as everyone else was exiting the room. He noticed that Jeff's math grades had been steadily declining. Mr. Smith pulled up a chair and sat next to Jeff while he was packing, and said:

"Talk to me, Jeff, how do you feel about today's math lesson?" "Can I be honest?" said Jeff. "Of course, there's no detention waiting based on your answer, Jeff," Mr. Smith said with a smirk on his face. "Tell me how you feel," he continued. "I hate it, Mr. Smith!" Jeff replied. "Why is that, Jeff?" Mr. Smith asked as he leaned back in his chair. Jeff started complaining: "It's so boring!" "It's just a bunch of numbers." "Why do I need to even know any of this?" When Jeff had finished, Mr. Smith asked him, "What do you want to be when you grow up Jeff?" Jeff shouted in excitement, "I want to be a firefighter. Just yesterday, I had a dream of saving someone from a burning building!" "That's a noble dream, Jeff." Mr. Smith said smiling. Jeff animatedly said, "Thanks!"

"Did you know time is very important to firefighters Jeff?" Mr. Smith asked. Jeff then stopped packing his backpack and gave his full attention to Mr. Smith. He stood there thinking for a moment before finally saying, "I didn't." Mr. Smith then smiled and said: "It's very important. It is so important that they have drills on doing tasks under a certain time. This is needed because a few seconds can mean the difference between someone living and dying." "I hadn't thought about that," Jeff said. Mr. Smith continued, "Some of the drills have to be done in under 5 minutes." Jeff looked at him in shock and said: "5 Minutes! It gets me excited just thinking about it!" Mr. Smith took a sip from his water bottle and continued: "While doing the drill, they are counting in their head to know where they are at, so they know when to pick up the pace at certain times. So, tell me Jeff, when the firefighter is doing a drill and 3 and a half minutes have gone by, how much time do they have left?" With a confused look on his face, Jeff replied: "Um um um. I don't know, Mr. Smith." Mr. Smith laughed and said: "They have 90 seconds left. At this mark, they are trained to pick up the pace. If it's done later, they may not be able to save as many people. If done too early, they risk burning themselves out. The firefighter has cultivated the ability to countdown and figure out how much time is left via subtraction. That is how I arrived at knowing that 90 seconds were left. I subtract the current time, which was 3 minutes and thirty seconds from the total time of the drill, which was 5 minutes." With widening eyes, Jeff said: "That's awesome! I wish I could do that one day." "So, do I!" Mr. Smith said, with a bigger smile than before.

"What was the subject for today's math lesson, Jeff?" said Mr. Smith. "How many seconds are in a minute and how to add and subtract them," Jeff said as his energy started to settle down. Mr. Smith looked at Jeff and raised his right eyebrow. "Oh, I get it," yelled Jeff. "Indeed, Jeff. What we learned today can not only help you be a successful firefighter one day but can also save someone's life," said Mr. Smith.

The next day, Jeff's attention to the subject of math was solid. He stared at the drawing board that Mr. Smith was demonstrating the lesson on as if it was his favorite TV show. They had a test the next week, and Jeff got an A+.

While fairly simple, this short story illustrates the linking of what you are learning and how it affects your goal. At the same time, it also affects your devotion to the learning of the subject. As all of this is more or less autonomous, this is important to understand. It should also be noted that the correlation of the math lesson and his goal of being a firefighter was direct. Mr. Smith could have easily just said the lesson would help him be a better firefighter and he wouldn't have been wrong, but would it still have had the same effect of getting Jeff interested? Based on the two factors named earlier, it would not have. By finding out what was his end goal, giving an example and relating it to the lesson, it had the intended effect of raising Jeff's interest in what he was learning.

We may grow up, but how our brain is wired never changes. This pattern of learning is still valid, even as we get older. What are the dynamics of why this is so effective, though? It is very effective because this approach used both sides of the human brain. You might be thinking, "Are you saying that this isn't the case most of the time in learning?" Unfortunately, it is often not. How exactly is it using both sides of your brain? To answer this, we have to know what the different sides of the brain do.

The Human Brain

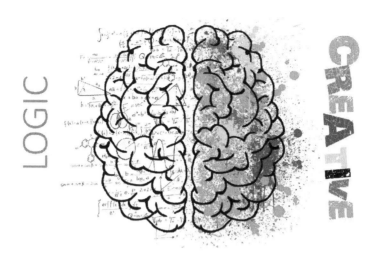

It is common knowledge that the left side of our brain is logical, and the right side is creative. While this is widely known, it is too broad to extract the jewels from. Here, we have a quote from an expert in behavior science, Ra Un Nefer Amen. In his book "Metu Neter Vol. 1: The great oracle of Tehuti and the Egyptian system of spiritual cultivation", pg 9, he states the following about the left and right sides of the brain: *"They are known as the left, and right hemispheres of the brain. To understand this subject, we must realize that underlying all mental activities are two sets of functions, one in charge of relating us, and the variety of things in our environment to each other, and to the whole, and the other function is in charge of separating us and the variety of things in our environment from each other."* This is the basis to which we derive the left side of our brain being responsible for logic and mathematics and the right side to arts, and relating to others. These 2 sides of the brain mean nothing without the 3rd part of the brain, commonly called the subconscious brain. This brain is connected to our limbic system, which is responsible for our emotions, and it plays a significant role in our ability to form memories. These right and left sides of our brain act as the car we use and the map to get to our goals, but a map and a car mean nothing if the car has no fuel. The 3rd brain serves as the fuel. Part of achieving true financial savviness is valuing the learning process as much as the goal itself. In the following pages, we will go into the functions of these 3 brains.

The Left Brain

The mid-left portion of the left side of our brain is where our analytical thinking lies. An analysis is defined as a detailed examination of the elements or structure of something. Without a structure or outline, there is nothing to analyze. This is another example of how the left and right brains work together to form our interpretation of reality (more on this when we get to the right brain). Now that we know what analysis is, we can look at what analytical thinking entails. Analytical thinking is the skill of performing an analysis. It involves the ability to apply logical thinking in order to break complex problems into their parts. Jumping back to our 3rd grader story, Mr. Smith knew of Jeff's lethargic mindset towards math, yet he pushed on to illustrate the value of knowing math. Mr. Smith (and later Jeff) figured out the firefighter had 90 seconds left via subtracting 3 minutes and 30 seconds from 5 minutes. They were using analysis, which is part of the left brain. Obviously, they didn't think "Hey, I'm going to use analysis now." This happened automatically based on the situation calling for that particular skill. The same applies to all parts of your brain.

The lower left part of your brain holds the skill of sequential thinking. This is the ability to come to the conclusion as to what the next step should be, based on what step you are in and the step that came before the current one. An example everyone can relate to is counting. If you want to take 10 steps and stop in the middle, you will know what step you're on by figuring out what step you were at last, to determine where you are. Then you deduct what step is next. I know this is the 5th step because the one before it was 4th. That means the next step will be the 6th step I take. 5 more to go! Smith's lessons were partly about seconds and minutes. He told Jeff that the drill had to be done in 90 seconds, not a minute and 30 seconds. To come to that conclusion, he had knowledge of the time system, so this allowed him to know the time left was between a minute and 2 minutes. His sequential thinking played a role in coming up with the deduction that there were 90 seconds left. Looking at the full picture, one part of the left brain divided the information into sections, and the other part put the sections into steps that let them come up with the answer. Whether this is a 3rd grader equation or accounting being done by a CPA, the process of the left brain remains the same. The only difference is how much that part of the brain is worked, and just like your muscles, they can be developed and made stronger if you give them daily exercise.

The Right Brain

The Midsection of the right side of the brain is how you form and use synthesis. Another word for this is systematic or holistic thinking. In all things, information included, there is an underlying theme that if you pay attention, you will see that it is always present. So, after enough exposure to enough things, in any given field, you see these themes enough to verbalize or write them down. After studying them, you realize that all ideas and information in the given area fits into or is related to these things you have verbalized. This is of such great use that you start using them in association with new information you find on topics in that field. When I went into GameStop to get a game, the employee there showed me the different sections they have setup. There is a section devoted just to sports games, but the sales associate took me to the shooter games section because they saw me staring at the Grand Theft Auto poster when I walked in the store. What separates them from other games in the store and what do they have in common? The underlying theme (in this case, it's pretty obvious) is that all of those games revolve around a sport, so this lays the groundwork for us to be what is known as categorical. It is the ability to put things in their proper category based on their interconnectedness. This part was demonstrated when they knew about the categories of minutes, seconds and how they both related and differed from each other. Seconds are part of the system of minutes but are not minutes in themselves. Without this part of the brain, they could have said 90 minutes and been entirely off. If we want to go to the extreme, they could have said, 90 hours, days, weeks, etc. It is this part of the brain that is categorial that allowed them to put things in the right place.

Since this is often subtle and takes exposure to the underlining theme many times before you catch on, one of the ways humanity teaches the development of this skill (and part of the brain, whether they realize it or not) is through stories. The story often carries the theme that is behind the scenes, and it is shown to the reader/view many times. Eventually, they catch on and begin to see where things are going since they have figured it out. Mr. Smith used this part of the brain by telling a story. The lesson was that math is essential in life. Throughout this story, he kept dropping hints to this conclusion, and it eventually hit Jeff. I hate to say this, but this is a very underutilized part of the brain in today's society. Often, a story can serve as a conduit to learning lessons from, so that you don't have to experience them directly. This saves you the time, energy, and effort it would take to do it and learn the lesson directly. I'm not saying that all lessons can or should be learned this way. It would be naive to think or even suggest that. Direct experiences have their place. So many people never make it to the big experiences because they burnout going through all these smaller ones. Why not learn the lessons of these smaller ones via a story? That way, you can deal with the bigger things at full speed instead of half power. This part of the brain is not to be underestimated.

This next one is not generally known or put into the right context by society in general. The lower right part of the right side of our brain is home to the ability to use congregative thinking, sometimes called congregative logic. I'm sure this thought is coming to your mind. "Logic? I thought the left brain is logical and the right is not!" This is partly true, but not completely. The way most people perceive logic is true, but the word logic has many definitions, and one of them is a particular way of thinking, which is often reasonable and based on sound judgment. The type of way of thinking and understanding is determined by the word that comes before the word logic, so the word congregative means to congregate, form together, or assemble. The right side of the brain works through pictures and visions. This part of the brain has the same logical step by step function as its lower left counterpart, yet the only difference is instead of words and numbers, it functions via pictures. I like to call it "puzzle logic." Someone who is very right-brained will be playing a scenario out in their head as you are talking to them. They are visualizing what you are saying step by step. If I was to tell this person, here's my day: I woke up, brushed my teeth, and had breakfast. Then I walked my dog and later that day, focused on doing my homework. They would see me doing the following:

1. Getting out of bed

2. Brushing my teeth

3. Eating breakfast (most likely what they consider breakfast is)

4. Walking a dog

5. Staring at the computer or paper

A visualization would accompany each step. Within each step and vision, the person feels what it would be like to be in that situation. "Must have been tiring to get out of bed. It was fun walking the dog. That homework seems so boring." Due to how this part of the brain functions, it can learn very well from examples. This is because examples engage this part of the brain. As the example is being heard, each part is being put in a step by step way via pictures, visions and feelings. During the elementary talking, Mr. Smith gave examples of how math was related to Jeff's career dream. If you recall, when he found out about the time details of the drill, he said "5 minutes! It gets me excited just thinking about it!" That was this part of the brain at work, picturing himself in that scenario and how it would feel, which, according to him, was exciting!

The Limbic system (called Subconscious Brain by some)

As mentioned before, the left brain can be seen as the map to get you to your goals. The right brain is your car. Are either of these useful to you without gas or fuel? This is what the limbic system is in the context of your goals. You can plan out how to reach your goal via your left brain and imagine the completion of your goal, and how good it feels via your right brain, but if the limbic system is not engaged, nothing will happen. To put this another way, you can tell a drunk about the health problems related to drinking too much (left brain), and show them pictures of a destroyed liver (right brain), but if the subconscious is not engaged, you might as well be talking to the wall. As mentioned before, this is the part of the brain where our emotions come from and make no mistake; if your feelings are not engaged towards your goals, they will not happen. This is what enables you to push when you don't want to, and to stay consistent when others are quitting (and trying to convince you also). It's what gives an emotional boost to the right and left brains, making them that much more effective. It's how you remember important things that are needed for your goals. People are saying something is too hard, and it is because this part of the brain is not engaged enough to store memories of what they need to achieve their goal.

So, why is it that some people have this brain engaged and others don't? Is it just as random as winning the lottery? Of course, not. People make goals all the time that they don't achieve. This is because the goal is far too broad and general. It often only exists so they can tell themselves they have a goal. If someone wants to make $100,000 a year as an entrepreneur, if they don't have the skills, the subconscious mind sees that as something that is beyond the person's reach, hence it does not engage. The limbic system is tied to the self-image a person holds of themselves. This is built up over time as we achieve more and more. To counter this, you must break down the specifics that it will take to reach your goal, so it starts to become more real and less of a fantasy. Doing this gives the subconscious brain something to latch on to.

After this, the goal must be seen as the ultimate goal, but it must be broken down into smaller obtainable goals. These 2 things are what separates the successful from the unsuccessful. Jeff had no interest in learning and likewise was not going to do good. Only after he learned the SPECIFICS of how math related to his goal was his subconscious brain engaged. He then deducted that this "math stuff" is necessary for the realization of his goal, so this, in turn, became a smaller goal on the way to achieving the ultimate goal, which was to be a firefighter. Then his emotions (the limbic system) were engaged and put to work. There are cases where a person can have a broad goal and achieve it, but usually, that person has spent years cultivating that ability via the process covered. There are ways to achieve a broad goal without doing the things mentioned, but this requires a lot of work with various techniques that interact directly with the subconscious brain. Such works go beyond the scope of this book, but if the reader is interested in that kind of study, they are encouraged to pick up "Kamitic Success" by Ra Un Nefer Amen. He goes into great detail about that process. In a nutshell, one must know that this brain MUST be engaged if they are to achieve their goals.

In summary, learning has many flavors, and depending on the person, one may be good for them while another may not be the best. Some people are right-brained and learn well-through images and stories. Others are left-brained and learn well through words and direct experience. Regardless of which one it is, it will bear little results if the subconscious mind is not engaged. Just because someone learns in a particular fashion doesn't mean you discard the other 2. By learning in ways that engage all 3, a person can learn based on their pattern and get reinforcement from the other 2. In this way, a person can learn a skill, system, or a way of thinking, and it can be absorbed into their long-term memory, giving them access to it anytime they need it.

Throughout this book, you will see at the end of most chapters, there will be assignments. These assignments are designed to cement the information that you'll be learning in each section using all 3 brains. There is a saying that goes that there is no better experience than the real thing. These assignments will help you implement the information and concepts presented in this book so that you can develop a way of thinking that will change your financial life for the better for the short term and years to come afterward! I know it may seem somewhat daunting to do assignments, but all of them directly contribute to building your financial person. In this way, you can break the habits that keep you in the quagmire we find ourselves in financially and replace them with practices that ensure you keep moving forward. Remember, in school at some point when you just stared at the paper instead of doing the assignment right away in class because on some level? You knew the information wouldn't help you make $$$. I'm happy to tell you you're going to experience the exact opposite here.

CHAPTER 2.

WHY IS MONEY SO X TO YOU?

"Money is an idea. It's whatever you think it is."

Robert Kiyosaki, multi-millionaire

This quote is excellent in illustrating what money is overall and how it is unique to everyone in their own way. For some, it is a tool that can be used to become educated. For others, it's something to have a good time with. Someone else may see it as what they need to survive. For many, it could be all of the above! From all over the world throughout history, it seemingly has meant various things to people in general. From Africa to Europe, to Asia, to name a few. So, if it means different things to different people, how have we managed to trade it for the duration of our existence? It could only be done by realizing that money has a certain level of value. The level of that value is determined by what the person wants to do with the money, so this gives birth to the notion that money is something that both parties of a trade value enough to exchange something for. What it is has fluctuated throughout history. At some point, it was gold, silver, platinum, etc. This time around, it is paper with art on it. What most people care about is the ability that money has to get them what they want or need. To fully understand this, we have to acknowledge that $$$ affects us. Many people try to ignore or get around this, but the simple fact is that money has the power to influence your emotional state. This can, and at some point, should not be the case, but we all start here, and you cannot rise above and manage something that you don't understand.

Money is a topic in an area of life that we're often thrown into. From a young age, we observe (whether we are aware of it or not) our parents or guardians. The face they make when they receive more of it. The look they have when some of it leaves them. How it impacted their relationships with others. Before we're even old enough to comprehend it, we develop our ways and responses of dealing with money. What these are is a combination of 2 things: Our personality and our upbringing.

A personality is a variety of different flavors. Some are introverted, and some are extroverted. Some are outgoing, and others are more reserved. Someone's personality is a combination of who they are at the core and how they adapt to their social environment. These factors play prominent roles in how we end up feeling about money. An outgoing person will generally spend money on certain things relating to their goals. Someone who is ambitious and is surrounded by other outgoing people will end up having that financial attribute further reinforced by his or her social environment. Someone more reserved, but surrounded by outgoing people, will feel pressure to be more like them. If this is the case, it could influence the way they spend money. They may change it, or that factor may further cement their current habits if they see these outgoing people always broke. Note that neither of these is bad. This is demonstrating how these 2 factors shape your personality.

Our upbringing, the 2nd, and more subtle one is the factor that usually happens without us even thinking about it. The 1st one, our personality, bears its own tangible results as we live life. I'm sure we can all think of instances where we screwed up financially and attributed it to "I see my friends do it" or "That's just the way I am." The 2nd one goes into territory we usually wouldn't look. For example, when you're under 10 years old, you take note of when your mother is happy. As you observe her, you can't help but notice when she is happy, she spends money. So, is it the fact that she is glad that makes her spend money, or that she has money is the reason why she is happy? Could either one of them be right? Just as we take note of when she's putting on a strong face, but you see under it that she is upset or sad. Interestingly enough, she doesn't spend money then. Are the two connected?

The above scenario is not universal. They could easily be flipped. Some spend money when they are down, and some are tight cashed when they are happy. The point is we very frequently repeat the emotional patterns that we see when we are little, and the action that comes with it. For example, let's take a stereotype that TV shows love to use. We see the female friend or protagonist that just got dumped by her boyfriend. At night time, we see her curled up on the couch, eating ice cream. Let's say we could jump into the show like in the movie "Fat Albert." We proceed to ask her:

"Why did you buy that ice cream and eat it now on the couch watching soaps?" She may say, "Me and my boyfriend broke up earlier today!" We say, "I'm sorry to hear that, but why did you feel the need to get that ice cream and eat it while doing this?" She says, "I don't know. I remember when I was little, when my mom had boyfriend problems, she would always buy ice cream and watch TV." Us: "So, your mom was sad?" Her: "Of course, she was." Us: Are you sad? Her: "I am. I guess I'm just like my mom."

What is the pattern? She learned the behavior to spend money when she is sad. Again, this is not saying whether this behavior is good or bad. The only way to determine if something is "Good or bad" is to have something to measure the situation by (more on this later). This example exists to show how we learn financial patterns from our deductions and observations when we are young. These factors, combined with our personality, give us our habits in general, and more importantly, our financial habits. So, many times than not, people ignore their emotional needs while trying to develop that financial savviness we've covered, so that they can get control of their spending and make more money. Ironically, this may not be the 100% solution for all people though. We'll take a look at that statement later in the book, but once these habits are formed, what gives them power though?

Energy, Time, Expectations

Think back to the 1st job you had. You got hired and started working. For those of you in the sales field, do you remember all of the preparation you did to perfect your presentation? You put the work in and you received your 1st paycheck, 1st commission or 1st sale. How did you feel? Unless you're a robot, I'm going to go out on a limb and say that you felt good, right? Even thinking back to that moment now may bring feelings of joy to you. Now, I want you to imagine that memory, but take out the part where you get your paycheck, commission or sale. You get a "Thanks." Now, how does that feel? I can already hear the mix of emotions. What causes these emotions in both cases? The fact that we have expectations and devoted our time and energy to the work is what charges the battery of our emotions. Let's take a closer look at these 3 things.

Energy

The word emotion is a shortened version of "energy in motion." Just like when you are running on a track in real life, heading towards a goal to cross the finish line. Going further into this metaphor, what happens to a runner who is running a 400-meter dash? They go through a series of steps. They take off with excitement as they build the momentum to reach their full speed. After reaching full speed, they wrestle with the challenge of maintaining the energy they've built up and not slowing down. They then start slowing down, and fight both physically and mentally to keep doing what they're doing. They are coming upon the last 100 meters, which was not visible to them during the whole race. The finish line wasn't in plain sight until now. It's staring right in front of them. The runner then gives all he/she has to cross the finish line in a final bust. Why not? The finish line is right over there. They blow past the finish line, and they have a sense of accomplishment.

When it comes to successfully achieving goals, it's no different. We experience a burst of excitement and start working towards the goal. This builds momentum up. Eventually, life gets in the way, and it becomes more of a challenge to keep that momentum built up. We know secretly inside of us that if we stop constantly contributing towards the goal, it will fade away into just an idea or thought. This causes us to push harder, and in pushing harder, we either maintain that momentum or slow down some. Which one of those happens usually depends on what's going on in our lives at that time. The goal finally reaches the point where we can see it, feel it, and borderline experience it, but we haven't quite crossed the finish line. So, we make a final burst as the pure vision and thought of reaching our goal reignites the momentum we had when we started and boom! We achieve our goal! Energy is the measure of the money and time we spend on things that we value.

Time

There are 24 hours in a day. Of those 24 hours, we sleep for a duration of them. Among the remaining hours, we either go to a job, run a business, go to school or manage an investment portfolio. Some people are doing all of these and more. We're not even going to go into if you have a relationship to balance. Once all of that is over with, we have free time. It goes without saying, our time is valuable! If you disagree, remember the last time you had to pay a visit to the DMV? Unless you have some kind of hook up (Which if you do, I envy you), almost every time you pay a visit to the DMV, you'll be there a few hours. What are you thinking about when you're there? The answers to this question could be limitless, but at some point, you're going to be thinking about what you could be doing instead of being there. Once that thought kicks in, a wicked feeling of anger or sadness kicks in as you feel like you're getting robbed of your valuable time. What makes this feeling go away (or at least it takes the sting out) is you are reaffirming that this has to be done because you need a service done here in order to drive. It is how we are initially wired. When too much of our time is put towards something we don't see an immediate payoff for, there is only one thing that stops that flustering and sad feeling. That thing is us reaffirming to ourselves that this time has to be spent in this way for us to achieve a need or want.

Anytime we perceive that we don't have to have the need or want, one of two things will happen. We stop investing that time, or we do so grudgingly, which causes a build-up of negative emotion that ends up coming out badly in some way. If you want a familiar scenario, this happens on jobs all the time. People who want or need a promotion start working extra hours. They put in overtime and volunteering to help with every little thing they can for the hopes of getting promoted. If they are not promoted in the time frame they deem is appropriate, the want or need starts getting shaky for them, and one of the two things mentioned before occurs. We then want to blame our boss, the company, the economy and everything else other than ourselves. Are these factors really to blame, or is it something with us that is causing all this?

Expectations

In most cases, what we expect from people and situations is based upon our previous experiences. We put expectations that we had of our old job on our current one. Expectations of what sustained our past relationships are projected in our current one. The thing with expectations is that it is internal. Few people are blunt enough to make their expectations about a person or scenario known. Regardless if their expectations are vocalized or not, they are the cause of frustration. The reason being is they are the milestones of our goals. For instance, someone who wants to be a manager one day expects to be an assistant manager. They know that it is on the way to the goal. When roadblocks appear in their way

36

on their journey to get there, that's a problem as far as they're concerned. The issue with having expectations is that they only serve their purpose when a goal is clearly defined. Many people have them, but don't even have a clear goal! That is why they become detrimental.

Take 2 people who have been dating for a few months. They have great chemistry and enjoy each other's company. One of them mentions that they should get their own place together. The other objects and says they don't have to. The asking person then gets upset. After they both calm down and talk, they both find out that the person asking wants to eventually get married, while it is not on the other person's mind. They hadn't even thought about it until it was brought up in this way. The goal of the person asking was to get married. Them moving in and living together was the next step towards that. It was an expectation. When the person encountered resistance, that's when the negative feelings started knocking.

So, you might be asking, "What's wrong with that?" There's nothing wrong with having goals and a vision on what needs to be done to achieve them. What causes so much emotional stress is when you put your expectations on the wrong things. Things in the world change and they may or may not be aligned with your agenda. When you put them on things or people that can change, you run the risk of getting disappointed. To get around this, we have to learn how to place our expectations on something that will always be the same; a constant variable. Something that is universal, undeviating, and objective. Let's say if the person had placed their expectation of having a win-win relationship, which is best for them both at all times, it would have had a much better outcome. The outcome could indeed be them parting ways, but it would be much less emotionally taxing because the expectation was based on the theme that all successful relationships are based on. If it reached the point where a win-win scenario is no longer possible, then it's time to move on. So, the question is, what is something that is a constant variable that I can base my expectations on and will get me to my goals without the risk of getting disappointed due to things changing? More on this later.

The 3rd thing is what causes us to have emotions (good or bad) when it comes to money. If we could put this 3rd thing into one word, what would fit the bill? Value!

The Value of Money

Whatever way you choose to secure your finances, it comes down to how much value you give something. Once you start putting energy into making money in some form, you'll at some point, gauge the amount of time you spend and weigh it against the amount of money you make. This, in turn, creates an expectation. As your skills improve and you get better and more efficient at the skills you're using, your expectations will rise if you are not financially settled. Many people settle with this scenario when they feel they should be making more. Some start looking for a way to do more of what they've been doing to increase their money. Others will seek more responsibility or skill development in exchange for more money. In a job setting, this could be seeking promotional opportunities or looking for another job that values your skillset more and shows it by paying increased money. In business, this could be looking into ways of expanding the business so that you can make more at the end of the day. Regardless of how you get your money, the time will come where you will want more of it for doing what you are doing. Whether or not you act on that desire is another thing entirely, but you'll only go after something that you place value on.

For you to gain power over something, you have to understand and respect its value. Many of us try to tell ourselves statements like "Money doesn't matter," or "Money is not important," or even "Money is not the most important thing in life." While money is not the most crucial thing in life, the impact it has on life cannot be ignored. If this were not true, then people would not be employed. Businesses would not charge for their services and products. When was the last time you saw someone barter something in exchange for what they want in a public place like a restaurant or a store? Money is needed to obtain essentials in society. What are the bare essentials? Food, clothing, and shelter, of course. What is required to obtain and maintain these? Nothing is stopping us from learning to farm and grow our food. Nothing is stopping us from going hunting to get food and clothing.

Money is used to buy things that you want. How do you get a new game console? How do you go on the vacation of your dreams? How do you live in houses you see in movies? How do you eat at restaurants you enjoy? Money plays a role in the obtainment of all of these and more. Sure, some of these can be acquired without pay, but the price is then measured in time and effort, which we usually don't want to give up. Money acts as a bridge that allows us to experience our wants and needs in a fast and convenient fashion. This fundamental fact must be respected if you are to value money enough to put in work for more of it. If you realize this and see its place in society, you've taken one step closer to gaining control over it.

Assignment for this chapter

Agreeing with something in principle is the 1st step, but until you apply the information in some form, it will always be just an idea with potential. Ask yourself the following questions: What can money do for me? If I had more time to myself, what would I do? If I had more money, what would I do? These questions provide the context for making the following list. On a sheet of paper, draw a line vertically down the middle and write the words "Financial needs" at the top on one side and "Financial wants" on the other side. What are your financial needs? What are the things you want and would do if you had more money? Keep in mind that money impacts your time. More money in some cases could mean more time to yourself and the ones you love. Write down your wants and needs. For example, my list would consist of the following:

Financial needs: A car, clothes, a home, a phone, a computer, food, and shoes.

Financial wants: Without money being on my mind or a deciding factor--the best car I can afford, the best quality food (100% organic) available, the most current gaming system, video games to play on that console, the ability to eat out at the best restaurants, the clothes I want, or start any business I want. Also, the ability to help those close to me financially when they need help.

I have more, but these are the most important. This list will come into play later in the book and will serve as the goals you have and the reasons why you picked up this book in the 1st place. When making this list, keep this in mind. The difference between a goal and an idea is that a goal is written down and reviewed regularly, while an idea exists only in our heads.

In summary, money at its core is a combination of your energy, time, and expectations. The extent to which the 3 play their roles depends on the value you place on money. Of course, putting value on money is not enough. The world is filled with people who want to be rich and genuinely desire money. Yet, the fact that they are not rich is proof that valuing money is not enough. It must be backed up by putting the needed work in and having a plan while also outlining what work needs to be done to get you to where you want to be financially. What is this plan or outline you speak of? That takes us into Chapter 3 and also the next phase.

Congratulations! You have completed Phase 1. When someone embarks on a journey, the 1st thing that must happen is the development of a tough-skinned mindset. You have moved one step closer to overcoming the wall of financial insecurity, which has its roots in the lack of control over one's earnings and spending ratio. Your skin should now be developed enough to protect you from damaging principles and concepts that are hazards to your cashflow. Speaking of cashflow, it's time to enter Phase 2 which covers income. How many different types of income are there? Which one is best for me? Can I successfully have more than one? These and many more answers are coming up in this phase. You will have the blueprint of how to increase your income. This is important because if you increase revenue without picking the type that is best for you, being successful can be even worse than failing. When done correctly, income will deliver you the activity, time, and fulfillment of your expectations that you want. When you go to the gym to work your arms and legs, you want them either bigger or stronger; maybe both. It's time to make that a reality for your financial person. Without any more hesitation, let us dive into it.

PHASE 2. INCOME

CHAPTER 3.

THE WILL TO RAISE INCOME

Part of being financially savvy is being able to raise your income at will. While many want to get their spending and earnings ratio in check, you sometimes simply have to make more money. Have you ever wondered why are people presented with ways to raise their income when they need or want it, but they don't? Perhaps this has been you a few times. I've certainly had my share of these scenarios when I was getting started financially. So, you may be thinking, "Why does this happen?" I could tell you but why reinvent the wheel when Robert Kiyosaki has already said it. "It is the why that gives you the power to do the how. The reason why most people do not do what they can do is because they do not have a strong enough why. Once you find the why, it is easy to find your own how." "Retire Young, Retire Rich," by Robert Kiyosaki. Right on, Robert! That is the balance between the method you use to reach your financial goals and the motivation to reach them, with the latter being the bigger of the two. The why behind something is the foundation for developing the will to push through the obstacles and achieve it.

I'm never going to forget something I saw back when I was driving for Ubereats. I arrived at a restaurant to pick up a delivery order. When I got there, a guy on crutches from Ghana came in and was waiting by me. We started talking for a little while I was waiting on my order. I then saw something that shocked me. I happened to look at his phone and noticed it had the Ubereats screen on it.

It turns out he was also an Ubereats driver! I learned from our conversation that he also had a full-time job in IT he worked during the day, and that he would deliver food for Ubereats at night. Shortly thereafter, a waitress gave me the order I was waiting on, so our conversation had to end. As I was exiting the restaurant, I was still partly in shock. Six months later, I was picking up at a Hooters, and when I walked in, I saw him again. He was still getting extra money with Ubereats. I was also still driving for Ubereats so I could have extra money to invest. I never asked him, but it's safe to say he must have had a strong "why" when it came to raising income. Take a step back and imagine someone who already has a full-time job in a high paying field and delivering food for extra money. On crutches, I might add. I didn't have to imagine it. I saw it and needless to say, it was quite inspirational. The will to raise one's income boils down to the desire for 1 or more of these things: Money, time, or opportunities. Why would a person want more money, time, or opportunities, though? That's what this chapter is all about.

If you ask anyone if they want more money, as mentioned earlier, most would say yes. When how is brought up, that's when you get those clueless or awkward eyes. What if someone had a method on how to increase their income? The gameplan is already laid out. All it takes is to put some energy into it. If asked if they would move forward, would they say yes? Would you say most people would run with it? Of course, they would! Who wouldn't? No one wants to leap into the unknown. The intriguing thing is that this happens every day in society. While the method and plan of how to do something are important, they will mean nothing if the plan has no action put into it. People sign up for network marketing teams and do nothing even when their upline has provided the blueprint. Many lose certifications they need to complete to work in specific fields. A person turns down a promotion even though they are perfectly qualified for it because they feel it's more work. These are just a few examples. I could go on and on with more, but that would be a book series in itself.

There is a line from the 1st Fantastic Four movie said by the Human Torch to Mr. Fantastic that explains it perfectly. "You need to control yourself and think before you act." Said Mr. Fantastic. The Human Torch replied, "See, that's your problem! You always think you never act!" Why is it that this is often the case with people? Why do some people succeed at raising their income where others didn't (and some made it look easy)? The answer is simple. The person had a strong enough trigger. This is the subtle behind the scenes, inside the core of the person that you don't see. You might be thinking, "What does he mean by trigger?" When someone gets some strong emotion, we say that xyz triggers them. The same applies here. Somewhere down the line, this person got triggered and keeps getting triggered on a consistent basis. By that knowledge, if I can find a way to get triggered, I'll have success at making more money. Are you expecting me to say it's more complicated than that? It isn't. That means our focus should go on that trigger if we want to increase income. You'll be glad to hear that's what this chapter is about.

Vigor and Passion: 2 Sides of the Same Coin

So, we have identified that we need the emotional trigger for success in raising our income, no matter the method. Without it, whatever our goals and dreams are, they will seem too big and out of our reach. This, in turn, makes the obstacles that stand between us and our goals seem too big to tackle. Imagine if the Flash superhero from the comics tried to fight the bad guys without his super speed. If you watch the TV show "The Flash," you don't have to imagine it since you saw it. The main villain of Season 5, Cicada, can dampen superpowers within a certain radius. On top of this, he more or less has the strength of Mon-

El (a race that rivals Superman's race of Kryptonians) from the comics. When the Flash would try to fight him at first, his powers would be dampened. This led to him getting beat up because he is a lightweight and Cicada is huge. The Flash has to rely on his speed in order to face his obstacles head-on. Trying to raise your income without these triggers is the same as the Flash trying to beat Cicada without the speed force. You will just get broken down, so you have to have those emotional triggers that fill you up with the energy to push through obstacles. It's when you enter this mode that things that seemed big simply aren't.

To do this, you have to spark two things in yourself: Vigor and Passion. Passion is born out of your wanting of something on a big enough scale that you can almost feel it when you are working towards it. It's that feeling that you find yourself sacrificing things that you value just for what you are seeking in some form or another. For example, I like to play video games, but I also want passive income through YouTube. I find myself sacrificing time that I would typically play Red Dead Redemption 2 for just making more videos because it gets me closer to my income goals. I enjoy making those videos as much as playing RDR2. Sometimes, even more. This is what passion is in its roots. It doesn't feel like you're sacrificing because you get your emotional kick from working towards your goal. Passion is the one that most are talking about when it comes to motivation to do things, and don't get me wrong, it is powerful, but vigor is just as powerful, only in the opposite way.

Vigor is the energy or force you feel based on your disgust, dislike or hate of something. These should not be pointed towards any one person, but when used in the right context, it becomes a powerful force. The best example of vigor for myself is the writing of this book. It upsets me that financial information, perspective, and tools are not provided to us at a young age by our education system. Unless your major in college is business or accounting, you are taught virtually nothing about money, finances, and strategic management of resources. You're just thrown into the "real-world" and expected to fend for yourself. Teachers' creativity to come up with ways to teach you about financial obstacles you'll encounter after your school days are inhibited by regulation and exceptions of grooming students to pass some tests instead of learning the skills with finances (or skills in general) needed in life. Even thinking about this is making me type faster to get this book out because of the large scale it is needed on and, I feel it shouldn't be that way. Everyone should be given the tools they need to be successful. This is one of the things that spark my vigor. It's rooted in my rejection of how things are conducted in the educational system when it comes to money.

Often, people have one or the other. Passion or vigor can take you far on their own, but if you want to unlock the true force capable of achieving your biggest financial goals and dreams, you'll need both. What's coming up next is just the blueprint to do it. As mentioned before, you need the trigger, but who said you couldn't have more than one? There are 3 types of triggers we can have, and the more you have, the stronger the force you have within you to work with.

The Selfish Trigger

Why do people work for money? Sure, there are circumstances where work is considered charity, but for the most part, you're selfish when you work for money. Disagree with me? Next time you get your paycheck, donate 100% of it to your local charity. If you're self-employed, give all the earnings you make from your efforts to your favorite nonprofit. Those voices in your head that are saying that I'm crazy are what proves my point. Society has somewhat conditioned us to feel bad about that part of ourselves. You hear things like,

"You shouldn't be so selfish" and "Think about someone other than yourself." If you put others down to serve your own needs and wants, this is wrong, but what if you are not? Does that mean there is nothing wrong with being selfish? You bet! It takes a level of selfishness to see your dreams come true.

We have to let go of that false principle that it's wrong to be selfish. It's only bad when you are putting yourself above others in some way. If you're not doing this, or better yet, if your selfish end goal helps others, then it's ok to feed that selfishness. I always ask myself, "Is what I am doing bettering myself? Is it hurting people in any way? Is it helping people in some way?" If I can answer "Yes, no, yes," then I'm good to go and what anyone thinks in terms of disagreement is irrelevant. I see the last question as a bonus. If the answer to that one is no, that's fine too. Some of my examples of a purely selfish trigger that fits what I've said is that I want to have a second home one day. It's bettering myself in the sense of that's what I want, and it's not hurting anyone. In this case, it's not helping anyone, but like I said, that's a bonus.

Some people can go very far off of this trigger when it comes to reaching their income goals. They see a world in the future based on the work they are doing now. They see a world that is an expansion of their means in one way or in multiple ways. Like mentioned before, passion and vigor are strong separately, but together, they are like a tidal wave. If you want to leverage this emotional trigger, you have to be clear about what YOU want in life. Once you have done this, you need to make the correlations on how money effects that. These must be wants and not needs. Needs bring out the survival in us, and not the abundance mindset that is needed here.

Assignment 1

Make a list of things that you appreciate in your life currently. Once this is done, think about how money affects these things. If you made more income, picture how you can have better versions of these or have more time to enjoy them. They do not have to be tangible things. They can be time-based too. For example, you appreciate the day of the week Saturday because you have the whole day to yourself, and don't have to go to work. What if more days of the week could be like Saturday? Feel free to take your time with this exercise. This is the foundation for how you will expand your means. You can't define what you want until you stop to value what you do have. As a tangible example, my list would be the following.

1. Time to myself

2. Video gaming and games

3. Reading

4. Spending time with friends

5. Creating things that help people (like this book)

6. Exercising

7. Dating

8. YouTube (Watching)

9. My outfits

10. Eating out

11. Building businesses

12. Food

13. TV

14. Helping people

If you've done this right, you'll have at least 10 things that you value in your life right now. If you don't, you'll need to spend more time on this exercise since this plays a big part in building this trigger.

Once you have done this, on another piece of paper, write down in list form what a world would look like if you reached your income goal. It's alright if your income goal is a little unclear right now. We will drill down into the specifics of it later. If you need inspiration, look at your value list and picture that on a bigger scale or in a much better-quality form. My list would be the following:

1.   More time to myself.

2.   More money for video games and the time to play them.

3.   More money for books and the time to listen/read them.

4.   More time to spend with friends. Having more money means we can do more fun and exciting activities together like rock climbing, vacationing, site seeing, etc.

5.   More time and resources to create better qualities things and projects for people.

6.   Being able to exercise when I want as opposed to having to exercise at certain times due to my schedule.

7.   Becoming a better-quality male so that I can date better quality women that I couldn't before.

8.   Having the free time to watch YouTube as long or short as I want.

9.   Not having money dictates the type of clothes I wear.

10.   Eating out at higher quality restaurants wherever and whenever I want without money even being on my mind.

11.   Building bigger businesses and partnering with others with similar goals.

12.   Affording the best food society has to offer (for me, the measurement is in terms of health).

13.   Having the time to watch TV if I want to.

14.   Having the time to help in more efficient ways.

15.   Paying people to do things I do not like doing.

16.   Getting back into MMA (Mixed Martial Arts) since I would have more free time.

17.   Attending more seminars on subjects I'm interested in.

18.   Affording more courses on subjects I'm weak on or want to become stronger.

Anytime you feel strongly about something you want, add it to this list. This is more of a conceptional thing, though. If I was walking through Target, and I see the new Battlefield game, I wouldn't add it to the list because it's already a part of number 2 for me. This is your passion list.

You'll now want to take that paper with this list on it and flip it over. It's time for your vigor list. Write down all of the things that you are NOT happy with in your material life. These are things that are, in most cases, obstructing your value list, hampering your passion list by default. My list would be the following:

Not having time to play video games as long as I want. Sometimes, I have to do things I don't care for when I would have preferred to keep playing for another hour or two.

Not having enough time to hang out with friends and keep those relationships fresh.

Not having the resources to do things on the type of scale I want. The budget dictates the scale.

Having to squeeze exercise in as opposed to doing it on a consistent schedule. Sometimes when I'm jogging, I wouldn't mind running longer due to being an ex-cross country runner, but I have to stick to a set amount because I have to do xyz.

Only having access to certain types of women to date. In this society, money often breeds success; hence, women that are successful in their careers are generally more confident and are of better quality to me. In order to get in that type of dating arena, my income needs to increase.

Not being able to tap into a better, more affluent social arena. Once again, my income would need to go up.

Having the taste to eat out but thinking about how it will affect the budget in the back of my mind.

Having a limited wardrobe.

Having to do tasks that I don't like but have to be done like color correction in video editing.

The same rules apply to this list. If you find yourself wanting to add to it, don't hesitate. These lists are the blueprint for developing that selfish trigger that provides the force to build you the financial foundation you want. Not all triggers are purely selfish, though. The next trigger is more on the selfless side.

The People Trigger

While our selfish goals are a nice fuel to have, the trigger of people benefiting from our goals is just as powerful. This trigger is not some grand mission statement aimed at improving humanity. In a way, it is the opposite. It is a concentrated perspective of how the realization of your goals will help a special someone or a select group of people. For most, this will be family and friends. A personal example for me is when my nephew in high school texted me one day, mentioning that he needed help with a school project. It was the type of project that required you to interact with a relative. I asked him when the project was due. He said it was due the next day and asked if I was free that evening. At the time, I was strapped with finishing a project of my own. I needed to finish producing a video for a client. The time had already been scheduled to complete the project then. I told him I might be able to come by before that evening, and I asked him when he'll get off from school. The time he gave was too late, so I wasn't available to help him because of the work I was doing for money. I didn't like the way that felt, and I told myself I would work towards having the type of life where that scenario would not repeat.

In this case, me achieving my goal of financial freedom (for me, having more residual income than expenses…making work optional), my family and friends would benefit from it because I would be free to not only help them when they need help but also spend time with them. This is the people trigger. Again, this trigger has its roots in your devotion to a person or a group of people. How does reaching your financial goal(s) help, or benefit those you care about the most? Both directly and indirectly?

Assignment 2

We all have people that are close to us. We also have people we enjoy spending time with. These could be clients, contractors, friends, family, associates, acquaintances, etc. Take 30 minutes to think about all the times that your making money had a positive effect on those close to you. Think of both direct and indirect ways. Being able to help a family member out by giving or lending them $100 is a direct example, but also focus on the indirect ways. If you put in overtime, the money made then lets you take Saturday off. You could then attend your friend's birthday party since you will be off and your income that week will stay the same. This is an example of an indirect way of you having money affects those close to you. Remember how it made you feel. The sense of pride that you were able to make it happen. The look on their faces that you're there for them or helping them. Remember how it made them feel. As memories are often buried deep in us, you must take the time to do this.

If you're listening to this book in the car, pause it and think about this until you reach your destination. Schedule 30 minutes of your time to make an eternal emotional investment into your financial future. The more memories of this you think of, the stronger the trigger will be later. After this step is done, you are going to entertain a vision where you have achieved a financial goal. If you have come up with your goal, picture it here. If you have not yet, don't worry. We will cover this later. Just imagine obtaining a financial goal that would bring a smile to your face. Further in this chapter, when you come up with your goal, you can repeat this part of the assignment with that goal.

Some examples are: I want to make $100,000 a year, I want to have a comfortable couch, I want to have a new bed, or I want more free time. You then need to focus on how obtaining this goal will help someone close to you directly or emotionally. Since you make $100,000 a year, you now take your whole family (mother, father, sisters, brothers, mate, and kids) on vacation. You see your kids playing video games and relaxing on the new couch. You and your significant other have a better time sleeping and doing the indoor Olympics on the new bed. Making more residual income lets you hang out with your friends. Picture their faces as you have a good time talking about the Texas Rangers game, or TV shows over dinner, or while you're bowling. If you've done this exercise to its fullest, you're probably feeling pretty sweet. You're now going to take all of those positive emotions and make a list of scenarios of how reaching your goal will benefit those close to you. You may find that some of your triggers from your selfish list may overlap here. That's ok. Just like before, I'll provide my list as an example. Mine, at this time in my life, would be the following:

1. Having the time to spend with my nieces and nephews.

2. Having the time to teach my family members directly what I know about money so that they can escape their financial quagmires.

3. Having the time to hang out with friends more.

4. Being able to make YouTube videos while being free of the influence of whether it will make enough money, and have it strictly based on what me and my audience wants.

5. Having the time to help friends with their businesses or investor endeavors (like assisting a friend record a video).

6. Looking visually appealing to that special someone via clothes, hairstyle, etc.

7. Having the funds and time to build businesses or projects together with friends.

8. The looks on the faces of the people in my close circle when they are invited to my first house warming party.

Just like the selfish trigger, this trigger has another side to it. The vigor spoke of before needs to be brought forward. Flip your list over and now write down all the times you missed out on those close to you because you didn't have the money or the time. The perfect example would be the situation with my nephew I mentioned earlier. My list would be as follows:

1. Not always being there for my nephews and niece.

2. Not spending as much time with my nephews and niece as I would like.

3. Not keeping in contact with my sisters as much as I should due to a hectic work schedule.

4. Not always being able to help my mom financially when I know she needs it.

5. Not being able to participate in projects due to time and resource restraints.

Once you're finished with these 2 lists, you will have what I call your people trigger. This trigger is where you get the old saying, "I'll do it just to see the look on your face." Of course, these should be genuine happy looks, and not raising eyebrows due to petty beefs. These are people that push through and reached their goals for their families and friends. The next and final trigger is similar to this one, but on a much bigger scale.

The Humanity Trigger

We all have a desire to be a part of something bigger than ourselves. Once we find that something, we feel obliged to contribute to that something in some shape or form. For some, it's donating money. Others give their time. For many, it's all of the above. We all have this desire to serve a mission or concept that is bigger than ourselves. To what extent that desire is flaring depends on us. The example that most are aware of or can relate to is charity. Giving to help maintain the charity or make it thrive while it serves others. There are many examples though, and they don't necessarily have to be that. It could be a nonprofit that has programs that feed the homeless. It could be a nonprofit organization that educates the community on skills they need, such as basic finances or how to apply for a job or assistance. These are examples that apply to society as a whole, but it can also be isolated to a particular group of people.

A Chinese organization that exists for the preservation of Chinese culture and teaching traditional Chinese medicine and history is an example of one of these. One personally for me is the BVSTX. It is a nonprofit that teaches and promotes the benefits of a plant-based or vegan diet. The key thing to note here is that it doesn't matter if society cares about it or not. The important thing is if they are fulfilling a mission on a big scale that you respect or care about, and by contributing to this entity of your choice, you feel you are doing your part for society (whether it be society as a whole or a smaller one). This is the trigger that vigor and passion are usually felt right away. You only need to focus on them. If I give to organizations that teach entrepreneurship, it is because I love entrepreneurship (Passion) and I also see that the lack of enough of them is making the economy suffer (Vigor).

Assignment 3

On a sheet of paper, draw 5 lines with space between them horizontally. Next, draw 4 lines vertically with space between them. The horizontal and vertical lines should cross at points on the paper, giving you a table. At the top, write the following phrases in the following order in each box at the top horizontally. Each word gets its own box. The words are "Problem," "society," "Positive emotion," "Negative emotion," and "Organization."

You'll probably conclude that these are categories and you're right. In the Problem category, write down all the things that you feel hold society back, or have to be improved on for us to keep progressing. Next, you'll want to repeat the same process for the other 4 categories. Note that the Society category could be an ethnic group, a nation, or all of humanity. That is up to you to decide. Feel free to have multiple things that serve different societies. For instance, the examples with the BVSTX and entrepreneurship are cases where humanity is the society. A more personal one would be the Chinese example before, as the society would be Chinese people. The emotional categories are meant to add fuel to the fire because you already know of the problem and who it is affecting, but you need a little kick for it to trigger. Some of the things I consider issues are:

1. Poor dieting (Humanity)

2. Lack of financial education (Humanity)

3. No copyright music available (YouTube community)

4. No free copyright photos available (Web community)

5. People getting assaulted (Humanity, but the trigger for me is greater for men since I'm a male)

For the sake of both our attention spans, I won't go through every category, but I'm sure you see the pattern.

The scale of this trigger is a lot bigger than the other two, so if your list is not as long, that's ok. Try your best to get at least 5 down. Once this is done, you want to spend at least an hour trying to find an organization that is currently working to solve this problem. These organizations don't have to be nonprofits. They just have to serve the mission statement of opposing the things on your list. Note that you will most likely have multiple organizations since the chance of finding one that is solving your whole list is close to nothing. If you're not sure where to start, try googling the problems. You'd be surprised how many people see that same problem, and some are taking action to do something about it.

Doing this assignment will make you aware of organizations or groups that are working to solve these problems you deem are major. This opens the door for this trigger to be developed if it isn't fully already, by giving money to these entities or volunteering your time.

Final assignment

Now that you have all the 3 triggers mapped out, you're now going to make a final list. We all have these triggers in us that has the potential to be developed. Based on our personality, though, one trigger is going to more or less be one that we are born with. Which trigger is that for you? Which one sparked the most energy when you made your list? If you're not sure which one it is, which trigger has the longest list? That's your personal trigger. With this trigger, you are going to pick 4 things (Yes, just 4) from your list and add them to this one. You may find this hard to do, but there are 4 things on that list that spark the most energy in you. If they don't now, they will later. After you do this, pick 6 items from your other two trigger lists, 3 from each. You should now have a list full of 10 things. This is your personal trigger list! Review this every night before bedtime or place it somewhere you can see it every day. Use it as the wallpaper on your phone, the screensaver on your computer, hang it on your bathroom wall and read it while brushing your teeth, etc.

The more focus this list gets, the stronger your will to raise income will be. Every time you feel those emotions come up when looking at this list, affirm to yourself that increasing your income goes towards solving this list. This list will be the reason you get through times you will consider hard. There is a lot of talk in the financial community about having a strong reason why you want the money or opportunity. They are saying that in hopes that something triggers in you, that will give you the will to raise your income. Rather than provide an in the moment heartfelt speech that will wear off a day afterward, I've given you the blueprint on how to develop a strong will toward making more money. This couldn't be more important because, without the will to earn more income, the following chapters will mean nothing in the grand scheme of things.

CHAPTER 4.

THE ART OF INCOME

Have you ever thought about what separates the rich from the poor? What separates someone successful with money versus someone who is not? To say it's a way of thinking would be the understatement of the year. On top of this, it doesn't leave much to consider. It is a way of thinking, but it's the program that runs in the background that allows that way of thinking. It's the structure that lets a person look at loads of information, and interoperate, use and arrive at a conclusion about it with ease. Sometimes, this way of thinking is passed down from one generation to the next in families. Other times, a person may pick up on it by being around people who use it. Occasionally, it is taught from one person to another directly via mentorship. More often than not, none of these are the case though. This way of thinking does not exist for many people because they weren't exposed to it.

Since for the most part, schools do not teach adequate information on money and finances; what we know about this subject is passed down from family. We then pick up more habits from our friends, and if no one in that circle has it, you won't learn it unless you actively seek it out. It is this thought process that once developed, it frees you from the anxiety and extreme attachment we have towards money. There are many people who are considered rich that have what some would find a controversial view on money. When interviewed, the interviewer always asks this question. "What would you do if you lost all your money or went broke?" While the wording of this question varies based on who is interviewing, it's always something eluding to this statement. Some of them respond with a cocky comment, but every once in a while, one will drop the secret. They always reply that they would have it all back within a certain time frame. A year, 3 years, 5 years, etc. How can they say that with a straight face? It's at this point that they have come to love and appreciate the joy that comes with this systematic thought process of making money. This leaves the money itself secondary. That isn't to say they don't enjoy the money. Of course, they do. Their confidence and joy become fixated in the system and themselves more so than the money. It is this element that this book will teach you.

You've probably heard this statement several times, but it doesn't decrease its validity. More money will not solve your financial problems. In some cases, it may put them on full display and make them worse. Until this element is developed and made part of you, there will always be a part of yourself that is insecure because deep down, you know if the money were to vanish somehow, you wouldn't know what to do. You will entertain thoughts of the money falling into your lap based on good luck, and having your financial foundation based on that is as dangerous as building a house on the slope of a hill with occasional earthquakes happening. I can honestly say that this is a good thing, though. It feels so liberating to know why things play out the way they do financially, and when money comes in, it was thanks to your efforts and financial savviness. Until this is developed, you won't have the earnings to spending ratio that you want. Trust me, when developed, it is invigorating, and if you apply the information you will learn in the following chapters, you will experience it on a daily basis.

The Information Age

We live in an age where information is no longer a barrier when it comes to making money or building wealth. While this is a strength of our current society, it is also a weakness. Since there is information about pretty much anything, there is no filter on what is valid and what is not. Something could be the worst idea on the planet, but if you don't know any better, it will appear just like the rest of the information. This is true for information in general and money is no exception. In the grand scheme of things though, it is more of a strength than a weakness. As long as you have your own system to filter the information, you can distinguish what is valid and what is not. It is basically what is good for your situation, and what isn't the best thing for you. The problem is getting a system that allows you to do this. I say problem in the sense of this is a problem in society at this time, but it won't be for you as it's coming up in this chapter.

As there is a lot of information out there, sometimes it seems that it is matched by all these opportunities to make money. These are even harder to filter or discard because as long as it is not unlawful, an opportunity may be a good one. It's just not right for you. We hear all the time from those around us that we need to do xyz to make more money, or that this way of earning money is wrong. How do they know what's best for us? Since money is an emotional subject, what works for one person may not work for you. So, who are they to tell you how to earn your $$$? These are the type of people that are trying to make a sales person get an administrative job and vice versa even though they are emotional opposites! One is a social and energetic way of making money, while the other is a more solitary behind the scene way. Do they feel what you feel when you are making money? Do they feel happy when making money one way, and dread making it another way? How would they know what's best for you? The truth is, they don't. It must ultimately be done by yourself. How do you do this yourself, though? Most of us are in touch with ourselves enough to know what we emotionally respond to (both positive and negative), but how do you practically use that so that you can capitalize off of your strengths and work on your weaknesses? Here is where that way of thinking, that systematic approach comes into play.

Money: The Masculine and Feminine

Everything in life has a duality to it: a masculine side and a feminine side. If you can see this, then you see the foundation for the system to be built. So, what are these sides, you say? To answer this, we have to look at what masculinity and femininity are. Although whole books can be written on these 2 subjects, we will summarize them by naming the key attributes of what they are at the core.

Masculinity is about mission, purpose, consistency, and breaking through barriers. To give an excellent visual, have you ever seen in the movies where the male lead is sitting at home just watching TV without employment. The wife doesn't care for it but says nothing because their situation isn't bad yet. After a few weeks, she finally gets mad and yells something to the effect of "Why don't you go get a job or make money? Bills are piling up." The man does not feel like it. In terms of masculinity, whether he feels like it or not is irrelevant. The concept of him getting over how he feels and doing what he has to do is masculine. This is an example of this concept in direct relation to money. His results are based on what he does today, not tomorrow or even last week. As you will see later in this chapter, this will play out in a major way.

Femininity is about love, feeling, comfort zones, patience, bonding with others, community, and opening up to receive. On the opposite side of the spectrum, remember in the movies when the female protagonist is going through some financial struggles? She reaffirms to herself that everything will be alright as long as she remains sincere and does her part. All of a sudden, seemingly out of nowhere, a way to address her problem comes. She got a tax refund when she thought she would owe. A friend shows up and gives her money as a gift. A buyer makes her a good offer for the car she's selling. These are a few examples, but they all have this in common. They are based on receiving something that helps or takes her out of that situation. These situations are usually based on what they have done in the past.

In relation to money, the person positions themselves to receive what they need and maintain their mental wellbeing in the meantime. That was a hard time for her, but she is a singer who performs locally. Things were just slow due to the season. She makes money doing what makes her feel good, which is what she loves doing. It's the exact opposite of the masculine approach, which demands action right now via activity to address the issue even if it means stepping outside his comfort zone, or if he isn't feeling it. One method is not better than the other. They are 2 sides of the same money coin.

Through this duality is born the way of thinking that allows people to see money in diverse ways instead of one big clump in a single word "Money." From here, we can look at how money is generated and categorize based on this duality. Knowing this is like a doctor knowing what a human body looks like on the outside. Sure, that helps and it's a start, but he or she will need greater detail to figure out what the problem is. Just as a doctor could not find out what is wrong with their patients without the knowledge of the anatomy of the human body, one cannot solve their money problems and see what works for them without the knowledge and structure of how income works. To find the answers to these questions, it's time to go into the anatomy of income.

What is Income Really?

"Money comes and goes, but if you have the education about how money works, you gain power over it and you can begin building wealth." Robert Kiyosaki. Since we are about to talk about income, the above quote seemed appropriate. At its roots though, what is income? It is a reward in terms of money for our efforts in a given situation. Based on what we just covered in terms of duality, would it surprise you that there are different types of income? I'm sure you've heard this before, right? Income made from just using your computer is different than income made doing physical labor. Is it though? If it is, in what way is it different strictly looking at the money and not the effort? Without the right tool to measure by, you can't tell how multiple incomes are different, or if they even are.

To get around this problem, what you measure income by has to be something that is built into the fundamentals of income itself. One thing that is never going to change is human nature and the attributes of masculinity and femininity. Using these as a measurement, the concept of income can be polarized based on the masculine and feminine characteristics discussed above. There are 2 types of income in this context: Orthodox income and unorthodox income. Orthodox being the masculine expression of income accumulation, and unorthodox being the feminine expression. First, let's go into the orthodox.

Orthodox Income

From the beginning of when humans started valuing things, we have had a trading system. I will give you this if you give me something in return. While money acts as the middleman nowadays, in its roots, it is still the same. You will give me "x" amount of money in exchange for me giving you this or doing something for you. For the longest time, this was how things were. Eventually, people realized that they needed the same things done over and over again. This sparked them thinking of a more efficient way to do the same thing. Every day, they have the same conversation with the same people about the same tasks being performed. What if we could do this without having that same conversation and negotiation? Just as they needed the same tasks done, the people doing the tasks required the same amount of money. They came together and had mutual feelings and thoughts. It is here where the concept of a contract was born. I will pay you this amount of money if you do these tasks for this number of hours. Inevitably, the duration of time for the assignments was extended as well as how long the contract would last.

Take, for instance, a baker who has a contract with the local blacksmith to make a certain amount of bread in exchange for a set amount of money every week for him. The deal lasts a year, and then it is renewed as long as everything is running smooth. This is steady income. It is coming in as long as you contribute to the things you agreed to for it. Sure, it can get repetitive and boring, but it is guaranteed income. It gets its "orthodox" label because people started seeing it as the most efficient way of handling working for money. Both parties knew what they would get, and there was no need for negotiation. In today's world, there are many forms of orthodox income. A few commonly known ones are:

1. Traditional employment

2. Running a big business (over 500 employees)

3. Dividends paid out to shareholders

Special note on orthodox income: This income's steady and predictable nature makes it measurable. That means that you can make plans around this income since it is constant and is expected to come in. How this relates to a budget, is that you can schedule to pay bills on specific dates with this money because of its predictable nature. The same goes for anything you want to spend money on. Due to the attributes we have mentioned, orthodox income is affected slowly unless for whatever reason the stream is cut off suddenly (a loss of employment, a business files for bankruptcy, etc.). This income rises gradually and falls slowly, giving you plenty of time to adapt to the change (whether it be positive or negative). For example, take someone who works at Kroger's. They get paid money per hour to do the tasks associated with their position. Every 6 months, they receive a 25-cent raise. This example demonstrates how orthodox income rises slowly. Hence, this is why it is measurable. This is both its greatest strength and greatest weakness. For something to be considered steady in this society, it has to have provided consistent money for the same or similar value for at least 6 months. When I was a process assistant at Amazon and an Uber driver, they were forms of this income.

Unorthodox Income

Continuing with the old school example. Before the days of contracts, products and services were exchanged by way of value or negotiation. That is where your old school so-called hustlers would fit in. This is income that is generated based on your own talent and your ability to communicate the value of that talent to others. Going back to the example used in the previous section, let's say that same blacksmith wants to entertain his family that night. He finds the local magician and explains to the magician what he wants. The magician then asks the blacksmith a few questions to get a feel for his personality, and what might make him laugh. She then gives him her rate for that night. In some cases, the blacksmith would pay for it, and enjoy the show that night.

In another scenario, the blacksmith might object, saying that it is too expensive. Clearly, the magician has the talent to entertain people. At this point, though, she must wrap that talent within another skill, i.e., the ability to communicate the value of entertainment so that the blacksmith will want to pay the amount she's asking. She then goes into how we feel less tense when we receive entertainment consistently. In some cases, it can prevent diseases caused by stress because you relax when you are being entertained. She goes on to explain how it disrupts the stress cycle, stopping it from building up into a problem. The blacksmith agrees and then pays. After a while, the magician rarely has to make that speech to anyone because word gets out around the village about the effect of her work. In other words, her work speaks for itself. If, at any point, she feels she is being under-compensated for the services provided, she can raise the price. On the opposite side of the spectrum, if she wants to get more clients, she could lower her cost.

This is unorthodox income. It consists of a primary talent that she does. In this case, the talent is entertainment and the ability to build and manage a system of valuing and giving out that talent. Some modern-day examples of this are:

1.   Direct sales

2.   Day traders

3.   Authors

What is fundamental to unorthodox income is that it is unsteady. There is no guarantee of anything solid that is there in terms of money and opportunity. That blacksmith, and many like him, love to get entertained, but they will not need that service every day or even every month. What if the magician approaches and he says, "No, thanks!"? How will the magician pay her bills? She will have to get out and hustle harder, get new clients, make more discounts, etc. Since her money is not sealed in any way, this is what she must do. On the same token, though, if she is willing to do this, she is in control of her income.

If the magician wants or needs to make more money, all she needs to do is put more energy into her system. Not everything she does results in the immediate desired outcome, but it still may do some good. Let's say she talks to the jewelry merchant and she isn't interested. The magician thanks her for her time and moves on. The merchant then remembers that she has a cousin who is depressed, and her act would be perfect for him. She then puts them in contact, and the magician gets a sale. The sale came from the cousin, not the merchant. She did not get what she wanted from the merchant, but nevertheless, it still moved her forward in her goal in another way.

What if that happened 10 times with different people? With this being the case, this income's unpredictable nature makes it very hard, sometimes impossible to measure. The cycles of this type of income can be very extreme. The income can rise or fall very fast due to things related to that industry. Soldiers have just come back from the war and want to be entertained with their families while they are home until they have to go back. Opportunities and this income skyrocket! The economy hits hard times, and all of a sudden, entertainment is secondary to basic survival needs. This income plummets. It can rise fast and fall fast. Naturally, this is why the potential for true wealth in terms of riches are in this type of income. It does not have a cap because it is practically unmeasurable vs. the orthodox that is measurable! Since it is so unpredictable, it is hard to plan or budget around it. This is why, in most cases, saving this income or reinvesting it is best. What makes this income also breaks it? Freelance video editing for clients or wellness assessments, as well as the tips I got when I was an Uber driver, are some of my personal examples of this type of income.

Special note on unorthodox income: It is generally known that if you give to others in the way of your time or money, it will come back to you in the form of $$$ or wealth. Donating to your local charity and maybe helping a friend move on your day off are some examples of giving your time or money. Most of the time, we can't quite put our finger on it, but once we do receive in some form, it clicks to us that "Oh, this must be happening because I gave or helped out with this, etc." Of course, this only occurs if you are giving for the sole sake of giving, seeking nothing in return. The universal law of giving and the universe will give back to you, even more, is found here. Unorthodox income is the conduit that this will come through.

As a few personal examples, I am on the board of the BVSTX, a vegan society that teaches those who want to learn how to transition successfully to a vegan diet. This means that I volunteer my time and sometimes money to this cause. Sometimes, it is emotionally challenging since I'm giving up my time, and it seemingly looks like I'm getting nothing in return. Then, I always notice a theme. When I was doing a lot of work for the BVSTX, after the workload had lightened or was over, I would seemingly out of nowhere, get more referrals from my current clients. This, of course, resulted in more sales, since I had more people to talk to about my products. I also noticed that my tips when I drove with Uber increased. These are forms of unorthodox income.

The Effort of Money

Unless you are doing something for a charity or nonprofit, you expect to be compensated for the work you do in one form or another at some point. These next 2 areas cover the management of that expectation. While you may get money immediately upon doing the work, other times, you do not. It could be days, weeks, months, or even years before you start to see the fruit of the seeds you planted. Just like before, your effort in regard to income has a masculine and feminine expression. Using effort as the measuring bar, the 2 types of income are active income and passive income.

Active income is the masculine expression of income, and passive is the feminine expression. It's important to note that one does not require less effort than the other. The only difference between the effort of the 2 is how it is measured. The effort of active income is rewarded right away in the short term. This means you get what you consider a lot for little time. Passive income, on the other hand, requires the same amount of effort, but you are not rewarded right away. Due to this being the case, the reward is stretched out over a longer period of time, or the prize is bigger since it comes in the future. So, what are the details of these? We'll start with the active income.

Active Income

When you were in school, think back to those tests that you had to take to move to the next grade level. Every few years, they would get a new name. Most likely, at some point, you ran across a story where someone had a job. They went into work, and then the plot progressed. We never stopped to think about why they were going to that job. The reason is that we see it all the time. What we see the most of, we tend not to question. That job that the protagonist was going to is a form of active income. To break down the phrase would be a little silly since it literally says what it is, and its relationship to money is within the words itself.

Both of the story examples given in the wealth sections were also active income, although different types (more on this later). What's important to note about this income is there is an expectation for immediate income before, during or upon work completion. Protocols (whether they be legal or social) are in place to make sure you get your money within that timeframe, and that the other party gets their work in that same timeframe. Here are some well-known forms of active income:

1. An Ubereats driver

2. A photographer

3. A General Motors employee

Special note one active income: It is this need for instant gratification that gives this income strength. Since everything is known upfront in terms of money and effort, you can quickly evaluate whether you want to proceed with pursuing the active income opportunity. That is the grounds for someone to reject a Walmart associate job because the pay does not meet their minimum expectations. On the same token, someone can accept the same position because they perceive the effort to be very small (the job isn't mentally taxing, etc.). If we could summarize this type of income, it is the ability to value what this income opportunity is for me TODAY in terms of money and effort. There is no speculation involved. Instant gratification is your friend here since it provides the foundation to value your energy and time.

When I design websites for my clients, this is a personal example of active income. If the client cannot pay, there is no service to be offered from me and vice versa. This is what makes it active. In order to earn active income work for you, you MUST have the ability to seek instant gratification. One must not come here with the mentality that what you do here will have benefits and rewards in the future. While that may be the case with some opportunities, what you are receiving now is what's important here.

Passive Income

You have most likely heard of this type of income before. Over the past few years, it has been running rampant all over the internet. It is used so much that it often serves as a buzz word just to get people to read or listen further. What determines if something is passive income or not is whether or not your CURRENT efforts are affecting this income. To put this another way, passive income is a result of the work you have done in the past, and you are receiving the reward(s) now. If you stop producing an effort and your income stops or declines, by definition, it is not passive income. I should also mention that we are covering the concept of this income, not the legal definition as far as taxes are concerned. That will be covered later in this book.

Going back to our scenario we've been using in this chapter, the blacksmith that we spoke of before goes to a building with his tools to forge weapons for his clients and the village. That building has everything he needs like iron and steel, but it's not free. He has to pay the owner of the building a fee every time he uses the building. The owner is receiving passive income from the blacksmith because he is not currently doing anything to generate that revenue. He is reaping the benefits from the past efforts he did. That building didn't drop out of the sky, and he happens to claim it. He had to either build it (which definitely took a lot of effort) or buy it. Even if he bought it, it took an effort to raise the money to buy it. The building owner is free to pursue other things or sit at home and watch the magician all day if he wanted to.

That money requires nothing or very little from the owner, when it comes in. A personal example for me is that I run a YouTube channel called "The App Lifestyle." It teaches people how to make money from their phone. For each person that watches a video, an ad pops up. If they watch a portion of it, I receive payment via Google AdSense, since I'm allowing the advertiser to run an ad on my video. This is passive income for me because I made the videos and I'm still enjoying the money coming in based on what I did, not what I'm doing. If I took a month off and went to the Caribbean for a vacation, this income wouldn't be affected. The 2nd job I ever worked was at a Walmart, which I worked for about 10 months. About a month after I quit, I woke up one day and checked my bank account, and I had $450.00 that come out of nowhere! When I checked the source, it said it came as a Walmart deposit. I went up there, and the manager said our store got a bonus due to our good sales over the past year. If you had been working for Walmart up to 6 months before the bonus was issued, you would get it. So, it wasn't a mistake that I got it. If that doesn't spell passive income, I don't know what will! Some commonly known examples of passive income are:

1. Rental income (generated from real estate)

2. Retirement income

3. Income generated from your downline in network marketing

Special note on passive income: Since this income comes in the future after you've done the work, you have to be mentally prepared for that. That means that you have to be willing to work for a duration of time knowing that you may not receive anything in the short term. How long is this duration of time? It depends on what it is you are working for. It could be months or even years. The App Lifestyle produces monthly passive income for me, but it took me 9 months of making YouTube videos basically for free until I could monetize my account. I knew this, and I was mentally ready for it. For something to not be considered long term, it needs to be more than a month. If it's less than a month, then it is active income. If something does take a minimal level of effort to maintain it, it can also fall under the category of passive income. One must have or develop the ability to DELAY gratification. This is the emotional core that passive income is built around. You must be able to set your expectations for what you are working for in the future. It is the emotional opposite of active income.

Orthodox income, unorthodox income, active income, and passive income are the 4 shaping factors around making money. You will find that every way possible of making money will contain at least 2 of these factors. You might be thinking "2 of these! Did I hear or read him?" Yes, you did. Just as you can't create a human being without a male and a female, every type of income is the combination of masculine and feminine.

It is great to know about these on their own, but as this book has been painting the theme so far, information serves a limited purpose until it is forged into a system. A system that allows you to quickly put things in their place and allows you to think on your feet, as well as deeply plan something out. The 4 types of income are part of a greater system: a system that covers anything related to earning money. It will allow you to see the dynamics and shaping factors of the 4 types of income streams. Each stream has its pros and cons. With this in mind, you can decide if you want multiple streams or just one, and if you want the first one, you can learn how to balance them based on your expectations and what you want or need. Ladies and gents, the time for suspense is over. It is time to introduce you to the money magnifier, which will be covered in the next chapter.

CHAPTER 5.

THE ANATOMY OF INCOME:

ENTER THE MONEY MAGNIFIER

"I feel that one of the most important lessons that can be learned is that what we "see" may be different than what is actually in front of us."

Mark Singer, CFP and President of Safe Harbor Retirement Planning

---

Often, we let our expectations of what we want blind us from seeing the reality of a situation. The subject of income is no exception. In fact, it happens very often. We want something to deliver on our expectations of a certain amount of money and time, not seeing that it may not be built in a way that can give us what we want. How would you be able to tell if this is the case and more importantly, how can you find or make something that can? It was teased in the last chapter, and it's time to go into it. You may recall at the beginning of this book, that there was a lot of focus on using both sides of your brain, i.e., putting things in their proper category, and the ability to use critical thinking. What you will read in this chapter will bring this into fruition.

What I call the "Money Magnifier" gives you the ability to put all things regarding income (the earning of it) in 1 of 4 categories. Each category has its pros and cons based on what you want. The cons of one category may not even be cons for you! On the same token, the pros of a category for you may sound good, but they aren't worth the cons. It all depends on what you want. This system will give you the ability to evaluate whether you want the type of income that section of the Money Magnifier offers.

The Money Magnifier

The Money Magnifier is a magnifying glass with 2 lines--one horizontal, and the other vertical. This produces a quadrant, and within each quadrant, there is a type of money or income stream. The Money Magnifier allows you to zoom in on an income stream, and once you've zoomed in, you can see which stream it is. On the same token, once you've zoomed in, you can choose to make that stream bigger by focusing more on it (moving closer) or you can decide to abandon it altogether.

The horizontal line represents your effort, and the degree it is concentrated for a particular result. The far left is where the effort reaches the expectation of wanting or needing active income. Active income, being on the far left, is also a metaphor for this income being somewhat synced with the left side of our brain, which is direct and has expectations, and focuses on the now or very near future. The same applies to money, which is why this income is on the far left.

The same applies to the far right based on your expectations and effort; it is passive income. Passive income, on the far right, is also a metaphor for the right side of the brain. Since this income doesn't hold tangible results immediately, you have to enjoy the work that you are doing. In most cases, you would do it in your free time even if money wasn't involved. The right brain deals with creativity, comfort, and feeling. This is why it is on the far right.

The vertical line represents your method of obtaining and building wealth. The top of the line is when your expectations are based on consistency, stability, workload cap (and by default, a cap on your money-making potential) and work balance, based on those attributes. It is orthodox or steady income. The orthodox income is at the top because you can see the top of something and can base your expectations on what you're seeing. You can also decide if it is worth going after based on what you want. This symbolizes this type of income's predictable and straight forward nature. Once you reach the top (whatever you consider the top to be), you have a whole foundation under you that will be there for quite some time. Symbolizing this income rising and falling slowly; hence, it makes a good foundation.

The bottom line of the vertical line is where your expectations are based on the unlimited potential to make money based on your talents, unpredictability, and immeasurability. This is unorthodox or unsteady income. It is at the bottom to symbolize that you often can't see the bottom of things. When you look in a well, you can't see the bottom. It is exciting because you know things are in there that you want, like gold in a mine, and things you need, like water in the well. On the same token, you can't measure how long it would take to reach that bottom. That symbolizes how this income can't be measured and this is why true wealth, in the form of how society views it, is here, and if you master the art of tapping into it, this is where the fortune is. On the same note, if you fall or something happens, there is nothing underneath you, thus symbolizing this type of income's erratic nature, making it risky and not the best foundation. It would make the fall pretty hard on you.

Based on how these lines intertwine, they produce sections of a quadrant. This quadrant contains the 4 types of money in the world. While this book focuses on the modern-day aspects of these money streams, they have and always will, exist in one form or another. This is because humans will always seek to make money in ways that are most accommodating to their goals and personality. Each quadrant has the attributes and the pros and cons of the 2 lines that make up the quadrant.

OA Income: (Orthodox Active Income)

At the top left of the Money Magnifier, we have OA income. This is the source of money that most are familiar with. It has the steady, predictable nature of orthodox income, and the activity of active income. It gives the advantage of getting consistent money coming in based on your current efforts. Many jobs nowadays are of this type of income. You show up to the job and work, which makes it active. You sign a bunch of paperwork during your hiring process, which is the terms and conditions. The paperwork states that you're expected to work a certain number of hours, and for doing so, you will receive X amount of money for those hours. These terms and conditions contain clauses protecting the worker's money earned from abuse and the employer's money that's paid to the worker. The employer could hire independent contractors to do the work, but their presence would not be guaranteed in most cases. On top of this, they would all have their individual rates. The employer opts in for an employee-model because they need activity on a consistent basis. The same applies to the employee.

This type of income is not limited to just employee jobs, although they do make a useful example for illustration. When I get in my car and drive on the Uber or UberEATS platform, I'm working for OA income. You may be thinking, "How so?" As long as the dynamics of what is bringing the income in is steady, and the service or product offered is engraved into society, it is OA income.

At this point, Uber is engraved in American society. People take Ubers to and from work, to and from the club, to events, etc. I could go on and on, but we would be here for days, and unless Uber wants to sponsor this book, I'm not going to give them any more free advertisement (#notsponsoredbyUber). People have sold their cars and just take rideshare everywhere. People order off of UberEATS due to convenience or laziness (if we're going to be 100% honest). You might be thinking, "Well, that's not engraved into society. If people stop being lazy, UberEATS demand could drop off. Does that make it another income and not OA?" While this technically is true, we have to look at what causes people to be lazy and want convenience when it comes to food? People work hard all day, 5 days a week in their jobs. This produces a situation for people to want comfort or to be lazy. Self-employed people often work harder. The factors that bring about the situation are all linked to the workforce and, we both know that's not going anywhere soon. Even if a change happened in the workplace like reduced hours with the same pay, that effect rippling down to the delivery industry would take quite an amount of time. Remember how I said this type of orthodox income rises and falls slowly? This is a perfect example of that. The pros of this income can be summarized as the following:

1. This income is steady.

2. Payment is immediate and based on the conditions of the terms; getting this amount of money for this number of hours. By immediate, it is obtained within a month of the work being done, which is due to the active portion of it.

3. It is consistent as long as you keep working.

4. Since it's steady, bills can be paid autonomously with it.

5. Fluctuations are low to nonexistent.

6. Since it rises and falls slowly, if this income starts to decrease, you have a lot of warning ahead of time before it reaches the point where it's problematic. You can use this to replace the stream or make changes to affect it for the better.

7. It doesn't take much time to see results in money when compared to the other 3 incomes. You start tomorrow, and you start earning the amount agreed to hourly or monthly.

8. Its structural nature shows a clear path to what you want. There is no guessing. Do this, and this will happen. That isn't saying the tasks are necessarily simple, but rather their relationship to the acquisition of money is clearly defined. If not, they are known very soon after starting. All the cards are on the table, and you can decide if you want to play the game or not.

Of course, everything has 2 sides. While those listed above are the pros, it has its share of cons:

1. Since it is steady and active, it can only go so far as there are only so many hours in a day. If you are "The sky is the limit" type of person, you won't like a cap being put on your earning potential.

2. There is no residual value in your work. You are paid once for the work you do. That's it. You have to stop working eventually. With no residual value being there, you're put in the position where if you don't work, you're not paid. That can unsettle some.

3. There is no potential to make money when you are not working.

4. It rises slowly. This can be a big con for some since they want their immediate efforts to have direct effects on their income.

5. Out of the 4, this is the income that can suddenly be cut due to circumstances out of your control. I got fired! I got laid off! Rideshare is being discontinued in my city, so I can't drive Uber (that actually did happen in London for a while).

6. With it being active, you usually have to deal with people to make money to a certain degree. If you are anti-social, this can be a turnoff.

7. The earning of it can be very robotic. Both the party paying and the party getting paid love predictability. That can be boring for some.

8. It can be demotivating for those who need big returns off of their effort to work harder, since the increase in income will be in what they consider the distant future.

9. Its structural nature can discourage creativity, because you have to stay in the bounds of protocols that are determined by the factors mentioned before that effects this income. Creativity is about free-flowing and going with the flow. Too much structure can constrict this process, and those that are or wish to use their creativity to make income will be off-put by this.

10. Overall, OA income is excellent for those that like guaranteed income based on a predetermined amount of work that they will do consistently. If this sounds appealing, then this might be the income you'll want to work for. If it doesn't, then one of the other three may be more your speed.

Special note on OA income: If you are going after this type of income, you need to respond emotionally to these 2 things. You must value the security in the steadiness that this income brings due to the shaping factors that were discussed earlier. You also have to seek instant gratification when it comes to payment for your efforts. This is not the quadrant for patience. Payment here is received within a month of the work being done. Often, this income has perks or benefits to it. Evaluate them and decide if they add value to your life and if they should be considered. Some benefits could be health insurance, shopping discounts, service perks, etc. When I worked at Amazon as a PA, I had access to health insurance and paid vacation. Also, since I'm an Uber driver, I can get a 22% discount on my phone bill with AT&T. Since I use AT&T, this has value to me.

UA: (Unorthodox Active Income)

At the bottom left of the Money Magnifier, we have UA income. What do you get when you combine the active approach to money and combine it with the unsteady and adventurous nature of unorthodox income? You get UA! When I was little, there was a United Artist theater that was practically around the corner from where we lived. I would sometimes call it UA for short. This acronym for this category reminds me of that. Ironically, the types of people I would see in these theaters were great examples of this type of income! Its active part makes it similar to OA income, but yet it's different. While that income had the structure of the orthodox, this does not. That means that the sky is the limit when it comes to how much you can make. The harder you work (active side), the more money you can earn (unorthodox side). Since it is not structured like OA income, the person here is free to use their creativity and talents to their full potential.

Here, you will find many people in professions that require a particular talent or skill. Actors are a fitting visual of this. An actor auditions for a role, and they get it. Then they appear in the next episode of the show to play their part. The actor then films for a few days, and then they are paid. Bam! They just made between $500 and $50,000 in a few days. What if they repeated that process for the whole month? How much would they make? What if they decided that a month of doing that would be a bit much. They repeat the process for 3 weeks, then take the last week off and relax. Remember the sky being the limit? This is the active part of it coming to play. Since there isn't a contract (a structure that outlines the time and work commitments long-term), how much they make is tied to how they work. This is UA's greatest strength and weakness. The actor also wasn't just having a string of good luck. Acting is a talent that they had to cultivate and eventually monetize to make money. The pros of UA income are the following:

1. The ability to use a talent to its fullest.

2. Being directly rewarded for hard work.

3. It can rise VERY fast quickly. Doing things you're talented at and enjoy brings a certain energy to you, and it draws customers, clients, or opportunities to you.

4. It is manageable. Work as hard or as little as you want. You're in control of your work to time ratio as long as you acknowledge the impact it has on your money.

5. This type of income often encourages creativity.

6. Its unpredictable nature can be exciting.

7. Since big money is possible, it can be very motivating.

8. This income is normally not as spread out. This means you often receive larger amounts of money in shorter time frames.

9. Societal factors can affect this income fast. Look at what happened to the magician in the last chapter. Revenue increased all of a sudden due to the soldiers coming back home wanting entertainment.

Now, it's time for, you guessed it, the cons:

1. There is no residual value for your work. You're paid once, and it's done.

2. If you stop working for whatever reason, your income stops. If you go on vacation, so does your income.

3. The lows can be as big as the highs.

4. Societal factors can affect this income fast. Just like those soldiers came home and wanted entertainment. What if another war happens, and they, along with many more, are drafted? That would affect the magician's income or how much time she would have to put in. The same type of scenario can happen to you if your income is coming from this quadrant.

5. The pressure of having to rely on your talent to make money can be off-putting to some. Some people associate work with doing something you don't care about.

6. UA Income is even more social then OA. If you're not social, don't have social skills, and don't want to develop them, it WILL affect your income for the negative here.

7. Payment is more of a short-term thing due to its immediate (active) and one-time (unsteady) nature. Money isn't stretched over a long period. In other words, you won't make this much money during these days and hours for the next X number of months. It's usually all paid right away or, at most, paid in intervals that will finish out by the end of the month.

People who enjoy UA income are those that can or enjoy using their talents to generate money. We often take this trait for granted when it should not be. Many people have a talent for things they enjoy doing and can make money doing so but choose not to. Have you met the boy or girl from church that can play an instrument really well? You ask them why they don't audition for a band or build a musical resume and eventually land a good gig. They don't want to. You ask them why, and they say they enjoy doing it. Once money is involved with it, they lose the enjoyment of doing it because of the stress and pressure. People who like this income, get a kick from using that talent to make money. This is the home of sales and anything that involves the refinement of talent to make money. Don't let the word talent intimidate you. Talent is simply something you are good at and enjoy doing. This ability can be monetized if you want it to.

Special note on UA income: Since the generation of this income is highly dependent on you and your talents, confidence is a must here. If you lack confidence, it needs to be developed. You are the star of the show, and you'll need that mentality to succeed. Security here is based on the confidence in one's self, talents, and ability to manage the two to achieve success.

With its active side in play, the emotional ability to seek instant gratification here is your friend. It brings everything to their conclusion as fast as possible, making things more efficient. Make sure to read the terms associated with how you make money here if the conditions are made by someone else. If you are making the terms, set up a down deposit before doing a service and receive the full amount after the service is completed. I still do this to this day. For my clients that I do video editing or website designing for, payment terms are set from the beginning. That could be receiving a partial payment and the rest upon completion or in rare cases, receiving the payment after the work has been done. If a product is offered, have the policies like refunding (or no refunding if that's what you want) in place. If it's all on the computer, automate as many steps as you can with technology. It is what I did when I ran my first health and wellness business. The theme of all these suggestions is to get the administrative things out of the way.

Having to attend to these administrative tasks can inhibit you from making money since they have to be done, but they don't make money themselves. I should also point out that regardless of the talent that you are leveraging here, the ability to reach out to people in certain positions and communicate the value of that talent to them for a fee is a skillset here as well. When I reached out to The Rideshare Guy publication about doing videos for them on Ubereats, I was using this skillset. I also do the same when I'm reaching out for potential sponsors for my YouTube channels. This should be noted as a talent within itself. It's something that may come naturally to some, but it can also be learned. If you don't want to do it though, you could always pay someone to do this part for you.

OP: (Orthodox Passive Income)

At the top right of the Money Magnifier, we have OP income. When I would watch a TV show or play a video game, sometimes someone would start off when you see them very weak. In a TV show, a character who is underdeveloped makes mistakes and doesn't think things through. In a video game, they are an average person. As their journey unfolds, they get better. The character in a show experiences growth and development. In the video game, you level the person up, and all of a sudden, they have gone through so much. They make great decisions and can beat anyone. The video game protagonist nearly takes no damage, and all his hits destroy his opponents. We would call these people OP, which stands for overpowered. In the TV show "The Arrow," the main character,

Oliver Queen (aka the Green Arrow), was overpowered when it came to his fighting ability after Season 5 aired. While he started out very good, the big bad for the season was always tougher. By the time Season 6 came, he had defeated the Dark Archer, DeathStroke, Ra's al Ghul and Prometheus, all very skilled fighters.

After that, even the show knows Oliver is overpowered at this point, and they start writing villains that try to hurt him emotionally since he's so OP. When you take the structure from the orthodox and combine it with passive, you get this! OP here stands for orthodox passive income, and it has the same potential to be overpowered, but just like the video game character starting, it starts out small. Effort must be put in knowing there won't be an immediate payoff. The payoff is in the future. Eventually, the concept of compounding starts to take place. The best thing about this is once it's built up to a certain point (however much you want it to be built up to), it will give you OP resources in terms of control and time since it is passive income!

The favorable sides of this income are:

1. The pay is steady.

2. It doesn't require much of anything to maintain once built.

3. It is scalable.

4. Usually, it doesn't require much interaction with people. If you don't like being social, this can be a pro.

5. Tends to appreciate with time, increasing cashflow.

6. It can make you money when you are not working (like when you're sleeping).

7. Since it's passive, you can spend your time on other things or reinvest the time into it to making the $$$ stream even stronger.

It pains me to do this, but we have to talk about the unfavorable side too:

1. The income is steady, which subjects it to rising and falling slowly.

2. You're not paid for your efforts today; you are in the future. This can be emotionally strange for some.

3. Since it's passive, it lacks the instant ability of active income to generate money fast. If you need more money in the moment, it's not going to come from here.

4. You can work hard and not see the instant results you want.

5. Since it is passive and rises slowly, you'll have to save for things you don't currently have the money for instead of being able to generate it in the short term.

6. If there are factors that are affecting people, systems, or technology this income uses, it can affect it (for the positive or negative). This can be a turn off since your income can be impacted, and it had nothing to do with you.

Passive income is something that is very hyped in society nowadays. People also tend to value consistency when it comes to money. Here, you get the best of both worlds. OP income is for those that are patient and can work while postponing the need for immediate results. It's like a fruit tree that you keep watering constantly. First, you plant the seed, then you have to keep nurturing and feeding it until one day, it is big enough to provide fruit. Then, it starts taking care of you. You see it progress from the day you planted the seed until it's towering above you. This tree analogy is almost literally how your relationship with this income is. Decide what it is going to be (plant the seed). Work on it consistently. What that consistency looks like is up to you. Do you want faster results? Work on it more often or longer in the intervals you do work on it (water the seed). Eventually, it grows into the money stream you want it to be, where it is accomplishing its purpose. Paying a bill, paying the car note, paying all expenses, it depends on your goals (the tree takes care of you). Then, OP will not only stand for orthodox passive income, but will also stand for overpowered on your financial statement!

Keep in mind that how far in the future you start receiving this income will vary depending on the source. For example, my YouTube channel produces monthly cashflow via Google AdSense. In the middle of each month, I receive the money I gained from the last month. In this case, the time range is from one month to when I started my channel, since videos I made back then are still making me money. Another example is someone's retirement. They receive nothing for years, but when the time hits, they are earning monthly cashflow. Both of these are OP income. Generally, a time frame that is less than a month would be considered active income and would fall under OA or UA income. The only exception is if the generation of the revenue gained in under a month is steady and requires little to no effort on your behalf.

Special note on OP income: What allows this income to be both passive and steady? An important question to ask yourself as this very question is the precursor to this type of income being born. For income to be both passive and steady, it must have something driving money via something to you. In reality, this income comes from the OA or UA categories and pays via a funnel in which you receive a portion of that income in the form of OP income. This funnel is either other people working, systems, or technology.

In many cases, it is more than one of these. To give a better mental picture, let us look at some known examples. In network marketing, you have the opportunity to build a downline. Your downline in network marketing are the people you recruit to be on your team. In many cases, you are receiving some form of OP income. That income is either coming from the customers or your downline. If from the customers, the bulk of that money goes to the employees of the company, which is OA income for them. The rest goes to you in the form of OP Income. If the money is coming from your downline, then they get a commission, which is often UA income for them. You get the remaining income, which is OP for you. We also can't forget that all of this is automated with technology and systems.

The App Lifestyle YouTube channel pays me monthly income. This didn't come about randomly. I created courses on how to be a successful Ubereats and Uber driver. People who want to make money with these services search for information on it. They come across one of my videos. They find value in it and decide to watch the whole course. They then enjoy the content so much that they sign up for my newsletter. Once signed up, the newsletter sends them other videos they may be interested in.

(YouTube payments in mid-April)

This is all passive income and is carried out by technology and a system. The best personal example of this is the Ubereats course I made on YouTube. The course teaches how to make the most money being an Ubereats driver. I did the content in a way that it is evergreen or continually relevant. This means that these videos will be in demand for quite some time. Someone searches for Ubereats training on YouTube. One of my videos pops up and they watch the whole course. Since the course is a system within itself, that's what makes it OP income. If this were not the case, it would be OA income. I watch TV show reviewers like airricksreloaded and pagey who talk about episodes of the DC shows like the Flash and Arrow. This content is only in demand for maybe a week after the episode airs. This would be an example of the same scenario (using YouTube) that would be OA income. It would be hard if not impossible, to convert to OP income because the nature of the content isn't evergreen. That is why a system is the foundation of OP income. In these examples, you see how other people, technology, and systems are fueling your income. This needs to be known and respected if you aim to build this type of income. Other people, systems, and technology need to be leveraged here.

UP: (Unorthodox Passive Income)

At the bottom right of the Money Magnifier, we have UP income. What comes to your mind when you hear UP? Probably first is that it is a word. Does that mean this income goes UP? No pun intended. Obviously, all 4 of these incomes can go up, but this one is special in the sense of you look UP at the sky waiting for the next grand opportunity to come down to you, and when it does, it delivers. You might be thinking, "That's an interesting metaphor." When you think about it though, it's not too surprising. Combining the sporadic, talent-driven nature of the unorthodox with the laid back, seemingly effortless theme of passive will get you UP or unorthodox passive income. This is the income that seems to come out of the blue, sometimes looking like it came out of nowhere. The best example I could give for myself of this is when Uber went public. As a public relation stunt to clean up their image for their upcoming IPO, they gave free money out to Uber drivers who had done a certain number of trips. I had done around 3,500 trips at that point, so I was qualified to receive this money.

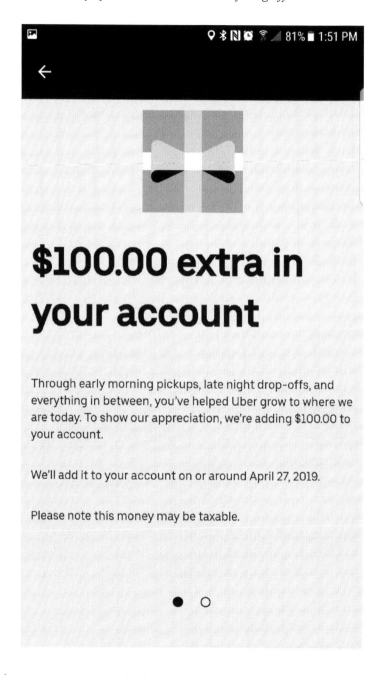

This money was not in the budget. I was genuinely (and pleasantly I might add) surprised. Partly, because I didn't think Uber was going to do something like this, but mostly because I simply hadn't planned for it. This income isn't steady, and technically, while I did earn it by having done the required number of trips, it can't be active unless I receive it within a month of doing those trips.

So, that makes it unsteady (unorthodox) and passive, hence this money went UP for me. Earlier in this book, you heard me speak of when I was previously working at Walmart and received money from them. Guess what type of income that was? You guessed it. It was UP.

In Chapter 4, I mentioned that what people consider blessings come through unorthodox income. If you have been following me so far, you know that there are 2 types of unorthodox income: UA and UP. These are the income streams they come from. Sadly, many people do not have the streams setup in this income to receive them through. These streams are many times the same thing that produces OP, except that they aren't forged into a system, thus making them unsteady.

Giving a real-life example: While I have just made wardrobe options like T-shirts, hoodies and sweaters for The App Lifestyle YouTube channel available (as shown below), I have not integrated them into my marketing system (email marketing, Facebook promotion, etc.). They are simply available. When someone purchases one, a system is in place to get them their merchandise. However, no system is in place for them to go to the online store to buy it. In other words, the supply side of the system is ready to go. A third-party company handles the making and shipping. The creation of the demand side of the system isn't in place. While you can click on the online store from YouTube or the website, without a complete system, earnings from these are pretty irregular and will be until I integrate them into my marketing system. Until I do, money from this gear is UP income.

The next question that follows is usually: Why wouldn't someone want to add these into the system? While I am going to add my App Lifestyle gear to the system, there are reasons why you might not want to add something to the system. Sometimes, it's easy to set up, but integrating them into your current system may be more trouble than it's worth. On the same token though, you're not going to pass UP on the opportunity to make more money (yes, pun intended). Other times, you may feel that adding it to the system may take away from other things in that system.

For example, if your system encompasses a specific niche of products, and you shoehorn something in that isn't part of that niche into your marketing system, then it may seem out of integrity with the brand you've built up. You could end up making the same amount of money or even less, because the other products distracted someone from the product they would have otherwise purchased. For argument's sake, let's say your earnings remained the same with this change. Your brand would have been stronger with just the niche products. These are just entrepreneurial examples, but as you saw with the Uber and Walmart examples, this income is not limited to entrepreneurship. If you're a grasshopper, you probably already jumped to the conclusion that this book is UP income for me. Indeed, it is.

The pros of UP income are below:

1. It can be a pleasant surprise. In my world, there is no such thing as too many of these!

2. Once set up, it can support the other incomes or yourself if it's set up on a big enough scale.

3. It can jump very high all of a sudden.

4. It is residual money.

5. Without the expectations of money coming right away, your creativity of making money is unchained.

6. Without the expectation placed on doing things for money, you feel free. What you do is not determined entirely on a price tag. You know it will pay off later. It can be mentally liberating.

You've noticed the pattern of this chapter. Let's cover the cons.

1. It can seem random, which doesn't breed much well for those that need to feel the work they're doing now is producing some result that can be measured.

2. It is the least consistent among the 4 types of incomes.

3. When you need money in the moment, the lack of active income is on full display.

4. It can be hard to scale.

5. Any work done will not show any money result until the future. Unlike OP income that starts producing small results that grow larger, this will show none until the day it hits. That can be demotivating to some.

This type of income is best generated by doing something you love or at the very least, enjoy doing. If you don't, you will find it hard to sustain. It should be something that you would be doing in your spare time, even if you were not getting paid. That's the scenario you will be looking at until it pays off. When you think about it though, this is the most liberating of the 4 incomes. People who earn income here tend to have a healthy outlook on life in general. Money often causes us to place expectations on things that probably shouldn't have them. "If I'm not getting paid for this, why am I here?" We are all subjected to these thoughts in the society we live in. That mentality has a place in matters that concern earning money, but not always in everyday life. It can be hard to turn off that part of us since it plays such a big role in society nowadays.

People who make money here tend to be detached from that scenario. Why do I say that? Think about it. They have cultivated the ability to do what they do without expecting a payoff anytime soon. If you can do that with earning money, you can do that in anything! The same applies to spending money. They know if they do their part, everything will even out and be taken care of. Like I mentioned before, the good deeds you do for others circles around and comes back to you in higher value in UA and UP income. While it comes in the form of opportunities in UA, it comes in through activity and money here.

Special note on UP income: Unorthodox passive income has the potential to make a person very wealthy. For most of us, though, we don't drop out of the sky with it built up. It is also the hardest among the 4 to measure or scale. With that being said, it still can be done, and that is the key to using it to build great wealth. Make a note or keep track of how much money this income brings you when it comes in. When it does happen, how much is it paying you? Did it pay more than the last time it came or less? These are indicators of the quality of work you are doing. Do everything in your power to make sure it keeps increasing. In my YouTube videos on The App Lifestyle, people sign up using my referral information. Once they use the app of choice enough, my payout can range from $5 to $500 per person. With Uber alone, I've made $12,845 so far, as shown below.

Screenshot of my Uber referral earnings

I did what I could to make sure that the stream per month kept rising — linking more of my videos together, creating a Facebook page and group for my exposure, holding live Q & As, etc. Last, but certainly not least, you need to have a plan for this income. I don't mean a plan for the exact amount, since you're not going to know the amount until it comes in for most cases. What I mean are the avenues that the income is coming through. You'll want to assign this money to fund something. If this income doesn't have a plan attached for it, it will simply disappear. UP income is best off being saved or wisely reinvested. The best way to reinvest UP income is through the vehicles that can increase your OP income or in ways that can boost the opportunities you have with UA income. If reinvesting into UA income, don't speculate. It should be spent in ways that have been proven to give you the desired result you want in the form of clients, opportunities, etc. There are also scenarios where work would be considered UA income, but for whatever reason, it doesn't sell or see results for over a year. When results do come from the work, that income would fall here.

These are the 4 income streams, corners or quadrants of The Money Magnifier. When earning income from one of these streams from an opportunity, you may notice that you could be receiving income that falls in more than one category. For example, as an Uber driver, I earn OA income from the money Uber pays me, but I also earn UA income in the form of tips. When this happens, which income do you categorize the opportunity as? You can categorize it in one of these two ways. You can pick the one that pays the most, or you can pick the one that you chose that opportunity for. I decided to be an Uber driver for the money Uber pays me, so I categorized it as OA income. It also happens to pay me more than the UA income in this case. Whichever method you choose, consider the other income stream as a bonus, but not the reason you're in the opportunity.

In conclusion, The Money Magnifier gives you the blueprint to income itself. More importantly, whenever you want to, or are given a chance to increase your income, you can decide which one of the 4 you want to grow based on what's going on in your life. So many times, I see people feel the need to make money. They try to increase their funds in not the best way given what's going on in their life. They get a 2nd part-time job (OA income) and end up miserable when they may have a talent (potential UA income) that can be monetized to make money. Making money that way leaves them more fulfilled and is an emotional change of pace from their full-time job. Another person may love to get that 2nd job because they enjoy the challenge, and the additional steady money it brings. An investor that receives dividends (OP income) gets paid just enough to pay the bills, but they want some spending money without sacrificing too much time. They can decide to write a book (UP and OP income) on their expertise as an investor, and that does the trick. Someone else with that same scenario may decide to get a part-time job (OA income) at Home Depot because it gives him steady spending money, and he always wanted to work there to learn some tricks of the trade when it comes to landscaping. Everyone's personality is different, as well as their emotional wants and needs. Using The Money Magnifier to identify what type of money something can give you will allow you to proceed or decline in a fast manner without wasting any of your time. It also increases your overall confidence in the arena of making money because you are now knowledgeable about the subject.

CHAPTER 6.

DISSECTING THE INCOMES YOU CHOOSE:

THE 5 MODERN WAYS OF MAKING MONEY

After reading about the 4 types of income, this question has undoubtedly popped in your mind. While some of these may lean closer to one or the other, it is not enough to generalize a particular type of income as being just one thing. We've covered the universal theme to income, that being The Money Magnifier. No matter what changes in society, the 4 income types will always be in play because they are linked to human emotions and expectations. It's now time to match it up with the modern-day methods that we use to make money. Making money in today's society falls into one of these 5 categories: Employee, Entrepreneur, Contractor, Investor, or Referrer/Affiliate.

Being an Employee

There is a good chance that you have lumped an employee into only being able to earn OA income. While there are more opportunities for this income here, that doesn't mean the other 3 aren't present. An employee can receive OA income from having a base pay that they are entitled to as part of the contract. They can also make commissions based on their performance, which is UA income. An insurance salesman employed by Geico is an example of this. That same employee can work there for 30 years and retire, receiving OP income. They could receive an unexpected bonus just like what happened to me at Walmart, earning UP income. You see how all 4 incomes could be earned?

What most people fail to do is to look for a job that has the opportunity for multiple types of income. People often settle for just OA income, with the opportunity for OP income later in the form of retirement. I say opportunity because companies that offer OP income in the future in retirement are unfortunately a dying breed. Retirement plans are switching from a defined benefit to defined contribution retirement plans. The difference is that the first one pays you a pension until you die, and in the second one, you only get back what you and your employer contribute (e.g., 401K). This kind of setup means that you could outlive your retirement. These are the names used for these in America, but they exist under different names in different places. I bring this up not to be professor gloom, but to point out that if you want to earn money as an employee, you need to know which income(s) you are working for in the job, and make sure it lines up with the income(s) and benefits you want. This could mean doing some research on the job and the company before you apply. Such precautions are needed nowadays due to the nature of the world we live in.

Being a Contractor

Being a contractor has become very popular among businesses and workers alike. Both parties find the "no strings attached in the long term" appealing. A contractor is anyone who receives money for their services according to the terms of the contract they signed. These are usually temporary and don't last longer than a year. At that point, the contract can be renewed. If the agreement is more than a year, it usually has contingencies in it that allow for scenarios to be managed between the contractor and the client. Its short term and unbinding nature are what makes it different from being an employee. On the flip side, this also means no benefits.

To give a real-life example, let's look at an industry we've all heard of before; the acting industry. An actor's pay varies depending on the role they have in the season of a show or movie. A series regular is an actor who will be in the majority of the season on a TV show. That means even if it's just for 30 seconds, they appear in most episodes. Their contract secures that they are paid a flat weekly rate, which is OA or steady active income. If they appear only a few times or in a few episodes that season, they will have either a guest-starring or recurring character role in that season. These contracts ensure they are paid on a per episode basis, which is UA or unsteady active income.

Many actors in movies have royalties on the movie sales after it leaves the theaters, which is OP or steady passive income. Eventually, the OP income will become less constant and turn into UP or unsteady passive income. Usually, at that point, they've already done another movie project or two and are starting the cycle over again. They are then getting paid OP income from the current movie and UP income from the previous one! This is just one of many examples of how being a contractor is in today's society.

Being an Entrepreneur

This is arguably the most desired of the 5, and here is the arena of raising capital. How that capital is raised is up to the entrepreneur. It could be sales. It could be raising investor money. It could be presenting business plans to banks for funding. I could go on and on about entrepreneurship, but there are plenty of people who have written full books on the subject. I'll instead give you a scenario that shows all 4 of the incomes that come into play here. Take someone who joins a network marketing company and begins selling the company's products. They cultivate their ability to sell, and their money goes through the roof. What type of income is this? It's UA or unsteady active income. The money is great, but they are tired of working so hard. It's time to pass the buck anyhow, so they start recruiting and teaching others their skills, and how to duplicate what they are doing. The teaching starts paying off, and their downline is producing results. Every time someone in their downline makes a sale, they earn residual income, which is OP or steady passive income. Initially, when they were teaching their downline, this income was OA or steady active because their downline was not self-sustaining yet. Occasionally, he hits a bonus as he and his team advanced through the ranks of the company. Sounds like UP or unsteady passive income, right?

While MLM (Multilevel Marketing) was used as an example here, the dynamics can be found in any business. The business owner has to run the operations of the company, which is OA. At first, they had to sell the products or services. What income is that? Yep, it's UA. Eventually, the business reaches the level where the systems are running the business and not the owner, which brings them OP income. They score a better distribution deal due to an economy-related factor. They get a larger volume at the same price as they were previously paying. They are able to sell more, and the additional profit from the extra products sold is UP income. This is why the dynamics of The Money Magnifier should be analyzed. Here, you will run into all 4 incomes. What's going to vary, is the percentages. It is best to have at least a ballpark figure of what these percentages are going to be, and projections on how to get there.

Being an Investor

Due to its convenience and passive nature, being an investor has gained a lot of spotlight over the years. Just like you may have assumptions about what type of income an employee can only earn, you may have preconceived thoughts about investing too. Like it only offers OP income. Obviously, it does, but the chance to earn the other income types in The Money Magnifier is here too. Just like being an entrepreneur, there are plenty of books dedicated to this subject, so I won't cover it in detail here. I will, however, go over the dynamics of being an investor concerning the 4 types of income streams.

To do this, let's take a look at the following example. A former teacher made her success by trading and investing. She is a former teacher because she now makes enough money doing these activities. She day trades on the stock market and has gotten good at noticing the patterns of the market. She buys low and sells high by using straddles, put options, and other trading tools she has at her disposal. This is UA or unsteady active income. She also owns stock in companies that pay dividends to shareholders, effectively receiving OP or steady passive income. Once every blue moon, one of her dividend stocks does well and has more profits than the usual payout to shareholders. They could use it to expand the company further. However, because there is no immediate need, they kick it to shareholders in the form of a special dividend. This is UP or unsteady passive income. Back when I first started investing, one of the companies I had shares in was AMC. I only had one share, but things were going very well due to their new subscription month movie pass they started. As a result, they gave a special dividend of $1.55 per share, which was much higher than the 0.20 cents per share they had been paying.

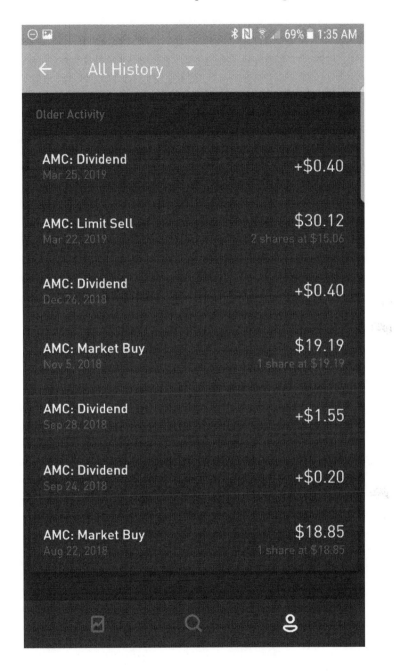

While I only had one share at the time, if I had more, that would have been a nice piece of change. OA or steady active income as an investor is practically unheard of and would be the exception of an income not fitting a way of making money. This is the place where you usually will have to pick a side of the fence, so to speak. Do you want active income or passive? Do you want to day trade or receive dividends? Do you want to flip properties or rent them out? Can you do both? Sure, but pick one initially and master it BEFORE moving on to the next one. Trying to learn both will typically get you nowhere. Both require very different and arguably opposite strategies.

Being a Referrer/Affiliate

I can't even describe how much I feel people have been sleeping on this way of making money! I put referrer and affiliate in the same category because at their roots, they are more or less the same thing. There are companies out there that don't want to spend money on a massive advertising budget. They've run the numbers and noticed that they could get similar results spending a portion of that advertising money. This leaves additional capital they can use to advertise in other ways. They don't want to hire sales associates to acquire more customers. They would have to offer them benefits, which is expensive. They could keep them part-time, but that would make the turnover rate high, which would put them back where they started. What do they do? They set up referral and affiliate programs! Everyone knows that word of mouth is the best form of advertising, and these companies would rather pay you a referral fee or affiliate commission for getting them more customers. They don't have to offer you benefits, and you can get paid just by recommending a service or product!

We will bring it home and look at me as an example. I've talked about the money I make off of Uber referrals before. I've actually gone to the mall before with the sole purpose of signing people up for Uber and Ubereats. What I was doing in that instance was raising UA Income. Referrals that come in from the YouTube channel were and are UP income. I am also signed up for various affiliate programs. Since I'm signed up with Amazon affiliates, I get a commission when someone clicks on the link of a video that talks about the product. This is OP income. I use many apps to invest in the stock market such as Robinhood, M1 Finance and Webull (all of which can be found at www.theapplifestyle.org). When someone clicks on the link to sign up for one of them, we both get money or something of value. If they sign up for Robinhood or Webull, we both get a share in a random company. If they sign up for M1 Finance, we both get $10.

Moving away from the YouTube channel, The App Lifestyle website is hosted with HostGator. I have an affiliate program with them where if someone clicks on my link and purchases a domain package, I'll get between $50 to $125 per person. That's all UP income. If a company doesn't have an affiliate program, reach out to them and try to set one up. If you are popular in an audience that fits their product, they may be willing to set one up just with you.

The best thing about this way of making money is that it can be structured to be which income you want it to be! That's why you want to look at the commission of the program. If the commission is high, it may make a better UA income source for you. If the money is low, maybe it's better as passive income (OP or UP), it's up to you, though. I didn't even cover referrals outside of online. When is the last time you had your taxes done? Do they have a referral program in place? My tax professional sends me $50 for everyone that I send to him to get their taxes done. If your tax professional doesn't have a referral program, I would consider finding someone who does. These are simple things we can do to make money off of referrals. What about the person that signed you up for health insurance? What about auto insurance? The list goes on and on!

How to Use this Information

All of this information serves to give you the right context of what you are getting into, or what you need to get into in order to fulfill what you want from money. Of course, if you can't see this information in the real world, it won't be useful. That's why the following assignment is so important. It will kickstart your abilities to see these shaping factors in the real world. Once you can see the shaping factors of financial opportunities, you can mold them to what you want, or decide to pass on them altogether.

Assignment 1

Using The Money Magnifier is just like any other skill. To maximize its effectiveness, you have to use it. The following is a list of professions and money-making opportunities. Correctly identify which type of income the profession or opportunity is offering you as well as which of the 5 types of ways the money is being made (employee, contractor, entrepreneur, investor, and referrer/affiliate). If you feel the opportunity has more than one income, pick the one that you see having the most money.

1. Someone is offered a job as a grocery stocker at Whole Foods Market.

2. A person that is good at playing video games decides to start a YouTube channel with the intent to monetize the channel and make money monthly via Google ads that he is paid on when someone clicks on his video.

3. A middle-aged woman is now retired from her job at General Motors.

4. A young man takes a course on how to wrap vehicles. He passes and is now certified to work in any garage that has jobs available. He goes to a wrapping garage and gets hired for a month's contract. He is paid on a per square foot basis, meaning that how much he is paid that day depends

on how much wrapping he did (No, I don't mean rapping in the music sense).

5. A student looking to earn money while in school decides to become a Postmates driver. She is paid per delivery, and the time it takes to complete it. The demand is steady.

6. A single mom wants to make money online on the side of her full-time job. She starts a blog about cosmology, a small passion of hers. In her blog, the products she talks about are available via third-party distributors, and her pictures on the blog contain affiliate links. This lets her earn a commission off each sale that is generated when someone makes a purchase on something she has talked about on her blog.

7. A successful web designer decides to write a book on the subject. It's available in paperback, E-book and audiobook form, and can be purchased on his website or on Amazon.

8. That same author half a year later decides to start an email list. When someone signs up for his email list from the website, they are sent information every few days via an email system that gives them helpful information and links back to his book. Is it still the same income?

9. A graduate out of college is offered a job at Allstate Insurance. They receive base pay and earn most of their money from commissions.

10. An actress is cast as a series regular on a new TV show.

11. A female student has heard her whole life that she has a beautiful singing voice. When she sings songs on the radio, you get confused, thinking she's the actual artist. She decides to follow her passion and hires a vocal coach. What income is she pursuing?

12. Someone with a passion for investing receives dividends from their stocks every quarter.

13. A life coach is asked to speak at an annual event in which the venue is paying him to come out and do public speaking.

14. An actor is guest-starring in 3 episodes of a season of a TV show.

15. A truck driver gets their CDL.

16. A small business owner employs 5 employees. The business is profitable, but it still requires the owner to run the day to day operations.

17. A high school student decides to go to welding school after graduation. After finishing, he hops from job to job as an independent contractor because he likes to keep moving. His contracts tend to go in 6-month intervals.

18. Someone gets hired as a seasonal associate at Amazon for a number of months.

19. An author receives royalties from the books they have written.

20. A popular DoorDash driver starts a YouTube channel to teach people how to become a door dasher. If people sign up with their code, they get between $50 to $500.

21. A freelance photographer takes pictures and puts them on iStock for a price. When people buy a photo, iStock receives a small commission, and the photographer keeps the rest.

22. A freelance writer is hired by Rev.com and transcribes the audio of YouTube videos into closed captions, so they appear as an option on the video.

23. Business is booming for an event planner.

24. A real estate investor receives monthly cashflow from his tenants.

25. That same real estate investor has a brother who flips properties instead of renting them.

26. A stockbroker earns a 7% commission off of the trades they perform for their affluent clients.

27. A YouTuber does a video that is sponsored by a company.

28. Someone buys a selection of growth stocks that don't pay dividends. They keep an eye on the company's news, earnings and market price. After 6 months, the shares have appreciated in value by 30% and the investor sells the stocks for a profit.

Review your answers below. If you were wrong on a few, don't beat yourself up. Did you know how to use an exercise machine when you first saw it? No, you were shown how to use it to make you stronger, but you first had to practice though. The same applies here.

Answers

1. OA; They receive money via direct deposit every 2 weeks. Type: Employee

2. OP; Once they do a video, they keep earning money from it on every view without much effort on their behalf. Type: Entrepreneur

3. OP; Cash flows in passively based on her 30 years of service. Type: Employee

4. UA; He is paid based on square foot. His pay is determined by his performance or ability to leverage his wrapping skills efficiently. Type: Contractor

5. OA; The factors of the delivery industry make it both steady and active. Type: Contractor

6. OP; She informs her audience about products and styles, and they use her link to buy the products. The shipping and making of these products are done without her having to do it. Type: Referral/Affiliate

7. UP; The book is merely available. There isn't any system around it. Otherwise, it would be OP. Type: Entrepreneur

8. OP; He has now built a system around it which leads people to the result he wants, changing it to OP instead of UP. Type: Entrepreneur

9. UA; Making money hinges on their talent or skill in the sales field. Type: Employee

10. OA; A series regular role means a role where they appear in almost every episode of that season in exchange for a flat rate weekly pay. Type: Contractor

11. UA; She's going into an industry where she'll be using her talent to generate money via concerts and song sales. Type: Entrepreneur

12. OP; The dividends provide steady and passive cashflow. Type: Investor

13. UA; The life coach is using his ability to speak publicly to generate income. Type: Entrepreneur

14. UA; They are paid for a quick-acting role that involves their talent. Type: Contractor

15. OA; They can use this to get a job driving 4 wheelers. Type: Employee

16. OA; The income requires them to be active and present, but it is also steady since the day-to-day operations he is running contribute to keeping money flowing through the business. Type: Entrepreneur

17. OA; Even though he is an independent contractor, his contract still run at 6 months. 6 months and up make it OA income. If it were under 6 months, it would be UA. Type: Contractor

18. Depends! For how many months? If over 6, it's OA. If under, it's UA. Type: Employee or contractor

19. OP; They are getting paid for past work. In these cases, their books. Type: Entrepreneur

20. UP; The referrals have no system that manages them coming in. This makes them UP. Type: Referral/Affiliate

21. UP; Same situation as 20. Type: Entrepreneur

22. OA; It's active, and the demand for the service keeps it steady. Type: Contractor

23. UA; This requires them to build a reputation and convince people that they can do what they can't or don't want to better. In other words, this is sales. Type: Entrepreneur

24. OP; Real estate kind of speaks for itself nowadays! Type: Investor

25. UA; Flipping properties is a skill in itself. It requires current work for current income, and it's not steady. In rare cases, it can be UP income if you fix the property up and it doesn't sell for over a year. Type: Investor

26. UA; It requires them to trade, which is a skill, and it's active. Type: Investor

27. UA or OA; It depends if the YouTuber booked a multi-month deal or if it's a one-off. Type: Entrepreneur

28. UP; The investor received no income via dividends but received a big payoff when they sold the stock. They also got their money back along with 30% of their investment.

How to Pick Which One(s) is Best for You?

So, which income(s) is best for me? That's a question that only you can answer. As you have undoubtedly seen by now, you can have all 4. Whether you do or not is up to you. In today's age, though, everyone should have at least 2. "How do I pick the 2?" You ask. First, you have to decide which of these 2 things are most important in your life today. Expression or stability? The line that goes horizontal on The Money Magnifier symbolizes this question. If the answer is stability, your desires at this time are pointing you towards the top or structured half of The Money Magnifier. Consistency is most important in your life right now when it comes to money. If the answer is expression, then your desires are pointing towards the bottom or expressive side of The Money Magnifier. The urge to express yourself and talents while getting paid in the process is vital to you right now.

The next question you ask is, what is more important between these 2: Time or activity? The vertical line of The Money Magnifier symbolizes this question. If your answer is time, you are leaning towards the right side or passive side of The Money Magnifier. For your reasons, time is more critical than direct control over earning money. If your answer is activity, then you are leaning towards the left or active side of The Money Magnifier. Direct control is necessary, and you are willing to sacrifice time to have control over your cashflow coming. If you followed this mental exercise, you will then have your answers. Those 2 answers will point towards the quadrant that is best for you to purse based on your desires and needs.

1. OA = Stability and activity

2. UA = Expression and activity

3. OP = Stability and Time

4. UP = Expression and Time

For the second income you choose, pick one above that you wouldn't mind or could live with. Note that for the secondary source of income, you don't have to be in love with it. You just have to like it enough to not mind doing it, and you obviously can't hate it.

Once you have a primary income (your first one) and a secondary income, review the 5 ways of making money and decide which one you want the income to come from. Note that both incomes don't have to come from the same way. For example, your primary income way can be as an employee, and your secondary one can be as an investor. Each method has pros and cons. Here are some things to keep in mind when picking your way(s): How much will I get taxed earning money this way? How complicated will taxes be earning income this way? Do the dynamics around this way attract me, or do I find it repelling? These are just a few questions that you need to ask yourself. In a later chapter, I will go over how to evaluate an opportunity, such as another income source, in great detail. For now, these questions are a good starting point.

Building the Income

Regardless of how many of these income streams you want, the best way to develop them is sequentially. This means that you need to build one up to a point, and then move on to another one. Trying to produce more than one at the same time will get you nowhere. On that same note, until you create an income stream to a certain point, it should not be counted as a stream in your budget. I have some income streams that are currently not big enough to mean anything yet. When I first signed up for the Amazon affiliate program, for the first few months, the money was less than $20. That's not enough to accomplish anything, so I did not count the stream. Only once an income source is big enough to pay for my smallest monthly expense will it be counted. I also didn't count my YouTube revenue income as a stream until it was enough to pay for my phone bill, which is $78. That is how you can scale your income streams from The Money Magnifier.

Every time an income reaches the threshold to pay for another expense, pause and decide if you want to keep growing it, or if you want to put your energy to another quadrant. Expenses also don't have to be bills. It could be a monthly subscription to an investor newsletter, your gym membership, monthly supplements you take to maintain your health, etc. As you watch your income(s) grow, you may find that you want to pursue other opportunities to make money in the same quadrant of The Money Magnifier. If you think you can manage it, feel free to. You can always scale back if it gets to be too much. Just follow the same expense measurement to keep it growing.

You can do this for individual sources in a quadrant, or you can do this for the whole quadrant. To illustrate this point, I have multiple sources of UP income, such as Uber referrals, Amazon affiliate commissions, and app referrals. I could count all of this as UP income when scaling or I could count them individually. If I counted all as UP, I would look at all of the income from these sources combined when scaling vs. if I counted them separately, I would scale them one by one. You can also create categories based on a certain way you make that income. For example, I put all the UP income I make from affiliate commissions under "Affiliate," instead of scaling them all individually. It all depends on how analytical or simple you want it.

You might be thinking, "All of this sounds great!" But, you need to see where you're to determine where to go. That's where this next assignment comes in.

Assignment 2

Now that you have learned the anatomy of income, it's time to see where you are currently. On a sheet of paper, draw The Money Magnifier. If you're not that artistic with a pencil (like me), you can write down the 4 money streams vertically. Next, write down all of the ways you currently earn money in each category. Remember, if the income isn't enough to pay for an expense, it shouldn't be counted. If some of them are blank, that's ok. You picked up this book to change that. For me, it is the following.

1. OA income: Ubereats, Uber driver

2. UA income: Video production/editing for clients, product sales

3. OP income: The App Lifestyle YouTube channel, this book

4. UP income: Affiliate commissions, Uber referrals

After you've done this, repeat this exercise and fill it with the methods that you ideally want to be earning money from in the future. Circle your desired primary and secondary income streams. If you're doing this on a computer, put an exclamation mark next to them. For me, it looks like this.

1. OA income: None

2. UA income: Public speaking engagements, seminars (occasionally)

3. OP income: YouTube channels, multiple books sales, rental income from real estate, stock dividends, online courses

4. UP income: App referrals, real estate, book sales from older books

This serves as a roadmap for where you are, and where you want to go. Don't feel bad if you couldn't come up with exact methods of how you want to produce your 2 streams. Just knowing which 2 streams you want puts you ahead of the pack. Keep your eyes open for the factors that shape the streams you desire, and if you see an opportunity that fits the bill, do some research on it. Talk to someone who is already making money that way and see what they like about it. If you could see yourself doing the same thing and enjoying it, put it on your future list and make arrangements to try and start building it.

As mentioned before, everyone should have at least 2 income streams in this day and age. You've decided which ones are best for you based on your wants and needs. It's time to get out there and find what streams you want! When starting with 2 streams, you'll find that the combination of them will produce advantages and things to consider. I will end this chapter with a brief counsel on each of them. When you see a symbol next to the income stream, it tells the state of it. Note that + stands for positive and - stands for negative. Positive means that the money is flowing in smoothly with no problems. Negative means that the stream is costing more to maintain, then it's putting out, whether it be money, time, or effort.

OA and UA

(+)OA and (+)UA: You are in much control of your income. The OA gives the foundation while the UA can be used to raise it quickly at will. The drawback is you are always in the equation when it comes to making money. Be sure to rest when it is needed to avoid burnout.

(+)OA and (-)UA: The foundation from the OA is strong, but expansion from the UA is stagnated. Consider replacing your UA income with another UA source. This is a sign that you are not enthusiastic about the opportunity to sustain it.

(-)OA and (+)UA: OA income is declining, or the effort to maintain it is increasing without the added value of the money increasing. After a while, this will compromise the flourishing of your UA income. UA income is very much tied to how you feel; hence, if you feel bad in any way, it will eventually decline. Redesign or renegotiate the terms of your OA income. If this cannot be done, seek another source before your UA income goes down with the sinking ship.

(-)OA and (-)UA: Too much effort is being put forth without the desired return in the wanted time frame. Consider taking a vacation from both. Reevaluate if they should be replaced or if it is time to seek other income streams.

OA and OP

(+)OA and (+)OP: Finances are all about stability. The OA income funds the OP, making it a great autonomous way of making money. This keeps both of them stable and slowly rising, and also makes for a solid financial foundation. It does mean that patience is needed since there is no way to raise money immediately. Learn to save for what you need/want, and you will do just great!

(+)OA and (-)OP: Money from the OA is being wasted on the OP. Money goes in and does not yield a result. This is a sign that speculation is occurring. Stop and find a better-proven model that will provide your OP with the potential to grow.

(-)OA and (+)OP: Effort or time in the OA is increasing. Your method of converting OA into OP income is working! The conditions of the OA are getting harder to maintain, though. Hold on! Take a vacation, take a few days off, get laid. Whatever you need to do to recover yourself and persevere. Eventually, your OP will become the greater of the 2, and you can scale back on the OA (go from full time to part time, higher a manager, work fewer hours, etc.).

(-)OA and (-)OP: OA effort or time increases while money put into the OP does nothing or little. Consider replacing one or more of these income streams. The stress produced from this scenario can lead to depression.

OA and UP

(+)OA and (+)UP: Steady cash combined with seemingly random money. Every time UP money comes in, you get a joyous feeling! A great balance between stability, activity and passive income when it comes to money.

(+)OA and (-)UP: The person (you) relies too much on the rain (UP). Rain is random. Drink from your bottle (OA) that you know is there instead of holding your mouth to the sky. Your expectations of the UP are too high for it at this stage in its development. Keep the OA as the primary provider. The UP is not developed enough to yield the results you seek. Learn to be patient and continue building the UP up (no pun intended).

(-)OA and (+)UP: UP is on the rise, and your valuation of the OA is on the decline. Don't take this as a sign to get rid of the OA. If you need to, replace it but don't get rid of it. The stability and activity it offers balances out the erratic nature of the UP.

(-)OA and (-)UP: The OA income is in danger of being cut off by you due to not valuing it enough or by another source causing you to put unreasonable expectations on the UP income. Replace the OA when the time is right, not because you are mad or scared.

UA and OP

(+)UA and (+)OP: UA is the rock, unmoved in terms of your confidence and ability to raise income. OP is the foundation in the making. Build the foundation as fast or as slow as you want!

(+)UA and (-)OP: Money put in the OP is not giving back what it should. This makes you question the system that the OP is based on. You're right to ask. Learn more about that industry and make the needed adjustments or hire someone to do it for you.

(-)UA and (+)OP: The system for steady passive income is solid and ready. There just isn't any paper to print. You lack the ability to increase your income at the desired rate so that you can have enough excess cash to put in the OP. Put the OP on hold and focus on cultivating the skills that you use to make money better. Better skills mean better quality output, which means people will pay more, or they will buy more. Only after doing this, will you have the $$$ to put into the OP, so that you can get that passive snowball going.

(-)UA and (-)OP: The desire to raise money and receive passive income is overshadowed by fear and laziness. These must be overcome if there will ever be a success. This could also be a sign that the reward of these streams is not enough at this time to push you to overcome the obstacles they offer. If this is the case, consider finding a different combination of streams.

OP and UP

(+)OP and (+)UP: The UP funds the OP. Part of the OP is used to set up more UPs. A formula that can make you very wealthy. These 2 combined, however, offer no way of generating income in the short term though. Learn to be thrifty so that you have saved cash to weather the dry periods until this funding cycle is established and your OP income can take care of you.

(-)OP and (+)UP: You have too many UP streams and not enough OP streams. This could also be that the UP set up is great, but the OP is not. The OP is the foundation. Pick some of your UP streams and systemize them to convert them into OP streams. The failing OP streams may be better as UP streams. A flip flop could be in order.

(+)OP and (-)UP: The OP is shouting, "Where's my money?" A sound system is set up, but there's no money going in it. This is the time where the good deeds you have done bring UP to you out of nowhere. If this isn't happening, it's a sign you're not giving enough back to society or those close to you in some form or fashion. There's only one way to fix that, right?

(-)OP and (-)UP: An inadequate system fails to provide results. The UP income dries up, and you're left out to dry. This scenario screams "Get a new system or OP!" In the meantime, you will need to retreat to the OA or UA and come back later when the timing is right.

UA and UP

(+)UA and (+)UP: Things just seem to come to you! Opportunities, gigs, money, everything is just popping right now! Respect the fact that everything has a cycle, and eventually, this activity high you're on will come to an end since there is no stability here. You know this, though. You thrive on the highs and weather the lows. Be thrifty so that the lows are mediums and the highs are super highs!

(-)UA and (+)UP: You making ends meet seems more luck than anything. Your UP income keeps bailing you out. Invest some of that UP income in increasing your talent or skill that brings you UA income. If that's maxed out, invest that money into something that will increase your confidence or help you be more aggressive in expanding the UA (Toastmasters, MMA classes, etc.).

(+)UA and (-)UP: Too much of your hard-earned UA income is being invested in questionable UP opportunities. Search for UP opportunities that have been proven to get you the level of money you want from it.

(-)UA and (-)UP: A Lack of ability to increase income, combined with the little income you receive is spent on UP opportunities that yield no tangible results. Here is the king of speculation. These are signs that the fear of loss is more than the joy of gain, or it's simply a lack of experience in both income streams. Fall back and enter student mode. Finding a mentor is a must!!

Are your financial person's arms as big as David Carter? If so, congrats! If not, don't sweat it. They'll get more prominent with practice. When you think about it, maybe you should sweat it since that's proof of work being done. Regardless, well done on completing Phase 2 and moving one step closer to becoming financially savvy. The task of climbing over the wall (financial insecurity) will require your person's arms and legs to be strong. We often place a lot of focus on cutting back on the spending part of finances, which is a factor, but you need to know how to increase income when you desire to.

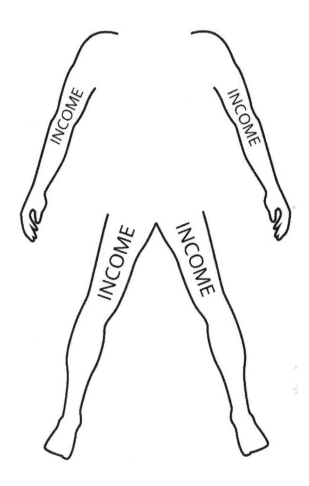

Are you ready to develop that financial core? It's time to move to the art of budgeting your money. Have you seen those people that think too much about money and then have ulcers? That's because their financial core is weak. Your digestion has a system that it uses to break things down, categorize it and send it where it needs to go to fill its purpose. A budget is no different. You just need the system for success that will divert the money you earn into the appropriate places to ensure you keep moving forward to your financial goals while at the same time, acting as a safeguard that protects you from the randomness of the financial world. Enough talk, let's get into it already!

PHASE 3. BUDGETING

CHAPTER 7.

THE BACKBONE OF FINANCIAL SUCCESS

If you've been following this book and doing the assignments in each chapter, you now have the tools to increase your income effectively. What happens when you grow your money, though? If you don't have a plan for the management of your money, it will slip through your fingers as quickly as you get it. Many people believe that their problem when it comes to $$$ is only making more of it. While this may be true in some cases, it often is not the only problem. If someone has an increase in their income (no matter how big or small), it will do them little to no good without money management and budgeting skills. Without these skills, one cannot be financially savvy, and will ultimately fail at keeping their earnings to spending ratio in check. That is what this phase and the next few chapters will be dedicated to. Giving you the perspective and skills needed to not only keep the money you earn but also budget it in a way that ensures you keep moving forward in all the areas of your financial life.

Think back to when you earned money for the first time. It could have been the paycheck from your first job, the first time you sold something, or perhaps the first time you completed a one-off task for a sum of money. Everyone's first time will be different, and I'm sure we all remember how it felt. Regardless of the circumstances, I'm going to go out on a limb and say that it felt good. You put in the work to earn for a reason, in this case, money, so that you could use it to contribute to your life in some form or fashion. Once that feeling wears off, another question or sometimes instinct comes to mind. What do I do with it? Based on what's going on in our life and the financial instinct of our personality (more on this in Phase 4), we want and often do one of the following things with that money: Spend it on bills, spend it on ourselves, invest it in some form, save it, donate it, or spend it on something business-related. Once we do that, we feel a certain sense of accomplishment. The cycle then repeats.

Without realizing it, we keep spending money in those ways because we are chasing that feeling of accomplishment. When we are forced to spend money in another way that is different from what we emotionally respond to, we don't like it. For example, someone who would rather spend money on themselves has to spend it on bills. Someone who would rather save money, spends money on themselves to maintain their sanity, feeling not so great about it in the process. Someone who would, instead of investing money, has to spend it on bills, and someone who feels secure paying bills, has to spend money on themselves, leaving an unsettling feeling. The examples could be endless, but you're most likely noticing the trend. We will go into where those feelings come from and why they are there in Phase 4. For now, let's look at the fact that before you even spend the money, we know it will be spent in one of those 6 ways.

There is nothing wrong with spending money on what you enjoy. The problem is that we often ignore or undervalue the other 6 (or 5 if you don't have a business). This puts us in a quagmire of not moving forward because a plan to spend money on all of these is needed to ensure your life keeps moving forward, not standing still and regrettable in some cases, moving backward.

The literal definition of a budget is an estimate of income and expenditures for a set period of time. This is more or less a plan for funds received and the spending of that income or resources. It's important to know that a budget can be a plan for the distribution of resources to achieve a result, and while money is a form of a resource, there are other forms. Since that goes beyond the scope of this book, we will focus on a budget concerning income and spending. Given we have identified the ways money can be spent, it's time to go into each of the following in detail: Spending of money on expenses, yourself, investments, savings, donations, and business.

Expenses

When we hear this word, our energy often goes down. It's likely because we see expenses as a necessary evil. Money has to go here; otherwise, life is going to get harder. While you're not wrong, take a second to think about how life would be without what the expense is paying for. What would life be like without your car? What would it be like without a place to stay? You would have to walk or ride a bike everywhere. You would have to find other means to convince the real estate owner that it's in his interest to let you stay there. What if you had to give him or her something every month instead of money? This month, I had to give my PS4. A month before that, my old computer. Before that, I had to give my favorite dining room set! What would life be like without your gym membership? Would you get fat because you couldn't go to the gym anymore? I could fill the rest of this book with examples of how life would be without expenses. This is brought up, so we can realize the role they play in our lives.

Ultimately, expenses need to be looked at from a form of appreciation. It's either looking at them like that or be stuck with that necessary evil feeling. I don't know about you, but I'd take that appreciation feeling over the other one any day of the week. What is an expense, though? The dictionary definition says it is the cost required for something. I'd take that a step further and apply that definition when it comes to things we need. I wouldn't consider me buying a new video game that month an expense, although it technically fits the textbook definition. This will be elaborated on in Phase 4.

There are 2 types of expenses. The first type is something that you pay for once, and it's done. If I take the toll road for an hour, a bill comes in the mail. I pay it, and it's done, unless I decide to take the toll road routinely, which I certainly will not! The second type of expense is the reoccurring expense. This type of expense keeps showing up for payment at a regular interval. You might be thinking these are monthly expenses. While monthly expenses are a type of reoccurring expense, they are not just limited to monthly ones. The biggest example of this is paying taxes. For most people, this is an annual expense, and for some, it is a quarterly one. Some common examples of reoccurring expenses are as follows:

1. Mortgage or rent payment

2. Car note

3. Utilities

4. Internet bill

5. Phone bill

6. Car insurance

7. Health insurance

8. Homeowner's insurance

These are just a few examples of many expenses, and while each person's expenses will vary depending on their situation, there are some universal expenses that most if not everyone has.

Living Expenses

Once you leave home and are on your own, you will likely have some kind of overall living expense to make each month. In most cases, this will be a mortgage or rent payment. Regardless of what it is, it's in your best interest to research and be informed on how what you are paying for is in your best interest at the time. For example, renting and owning, while both are a living expense, they are different and have very different pros and cons. A person financing a house with a 30-year mortgage will slowly build equity in the house as they make their payments. This means that if they decide to sell in the future, they can get money out of the deal. If the house is paid off, they will no longer have that living expense to deal with. They could even rent the house out and make rental income if they wanted to. On the flip side, the house is theirs, so when something goes wrong with the property, they are responsible for fixing it. That 30-year mortgage also ties their hands. If they break that agreement for whatever reason, it will affect their credit report, which can inhibit their buying decisions going forward. Is owning a home worth the pros and cons of it?

Turning it around a bit, a person who rents a house has no long-term strings attached. If they get a better job offer in a new city, it is relatively easy to move on from that property and move to their new work location. The landlord is responsible for the upkeep of much of the property, leaving these tasks off the person's mind. On the other side, the payments they are making contribute no long-term value since they do not own the property, and if they wanted to make changes to the place, they couldn't. Renting also has its pros and cons.

These examples are simple and don't go into the details, but they are used to illustrate the point that a living expense is necessary. But, which one is best? Someone who is somewhat of a nomad, putting in applications for a job in their field, is ready to get up and relocate their whole life if the right job offer comes may find more value in renting. Someone who is more stable and looking to raise a family may find owning more valuable. The key is, that thought is put into how this needed expense serves your interests. We often overlook doing this because we dread expenses so much. Once you look at expenses from the perspective mentioned above, you start to see how this expense is serving you. This also paves the foundation for you to see how the same type of expense that serves a purpose may serve your needs better in a different form and sometimes for around the same price.

Car Note

Buying a car in cash is fantastic, but in many cases, it has to be financed. Or isn't it? Is it more practical to save the money and buy a cash car? Does it make more sense to finance the car? These are the questions you should be asking yourself. If you do finance a car, should it be a new or used car? How will that decision affect other expenses down the line (oil changes, maintenance, replacing brakes, etc.)? These things may be a more significant factor in a used car, but more times than not, a used car is cheaper than a new one. Is the $$$ difference between the new and used one going to make up for the depreciation of the used car? On top of these, what will the interest be if you do finance? Only you can decide this, but these questions have to be on your mind for you to make an informed decision.

Liabilities

All of these questions lead to this word if they haven't been mostly positive. The popularized definition of a liability is something that takes cash out of your pocket. Some see liabilities as reoccurring expenses. They technically are and feel free to label them as such. Since by definition, a liability is an expense, you will hear me referring to them as reoccurring expenses or just expenses for the duration of this book. The thing to remember here is that there are needed expenses and unneeded expenses. This is not saying you should not have unnecessary expenses. You just want to keep them manageable and to a minimum until your income increases enough to justify expanding your means. It is that very behavior that creates an imbalance in a person's earnings to spending ratio, likewise causing financial problems. Paying for an expensive golf club membership when you can barely make rent payments is a visual of this scenario. On the flip side, if you are doing well for yourself, with steady cashflow every month meeting your monthly expenses, you have a savings and modest investments, then something like that isn't bad. It's just expanding your means and may even serve as motivation to maintain it (more on this in the next phase).

There is nothing wrong with getting things that allow you to enjoy life. These should be obtained after you've acquired the income stream that can pay for these things. Depending on which of the 4 streams it is, the approach for paying for something can be different. Will it be better to pay these things off in payments or save and buy in cash? That depends on your personality. Again, this is covered in Phase 4.

In a nutshell, expenses are needed to live in today's society. We have the freedom to choose which ones we want, and since we do, it's in our best interest to educate ourselves about the ones that are best for our situation. To do this, we have to be familiar with the dynamics of our situation, and how these needed expenses affect it--for better or worse. While there are different types of expenses, they all fall into one of these categories: Survival expenses, luxury expenses, and investor expenses. These are covered in more detail in Chapter 9.

Savings

It is a concept that is as old as money itself. "You should always have savings. You never know when a rainy day will come." Nowadays, the stakes are higher than just a rainy day. Things come out of nowhere, and these things cost money. The sink is leaking. The transmission in my car needs to be replaced. There are foundation problems with the house that will cost X amount of dollars to fix. If you haven't encountered any of these, I'm sure you have your own list of unexpected financial expenses that come seemingly out of nowhere. Sometimes, they don't exactly come out of nowhere. You know they will eventually happen, but not precisely when.

Regardless of which one of these it is, they aren't in the budget. So, where does the money to pay for it come from? It either comes from savings or from you going out and making more money. Even if you can make the money, often, these things are time-sensitive and require you to pay now (as in, right that moment). Having shingles on your roof needing repair during the rainy season isn't exactly something you can sleep on unless you want to star in your own Aquaman film. You can always replace the money soon after, but the immediate cash must come from somewhere. On top of this, there is money that just isn't going into the other categories. By definition, it goes here. Later down the line, you can use the money for something. It couldn't hurt, right? Or, could it? This is what I mean by 'today, the stakes are higher.' To cover this point, we have to go into a little something called inflation.

Inflation

What is inflation, you might be asking? The textbook definition (that textbook being the dictionary) is the general increase in prices and fall in the purchasing value of money. Translating that into modern terms, inflation is the devaluing of currency, which results in more of that currency being needed to buy things of value. This means that your money is worthless in terms of purchasing power. A famous example of this is looking at a loaf of bread. How much did it cost in 1930? Take a second to guess as it can be quite surprising. It cost 0.09 cents. That seems crazy, right? In 2019, how much does a loaf of bread cost? I'm sure you're familiar with this to some degree, but on average, that bread costs $2.50. As you see, the purchasing power of the money supply has decreased.

What does this have to do with saving, though? Everything! Since money is getting eaten away every day by inflation, when your $$$ is sitting still, you are actually losing money. To illustrate this point, let's take a look at having $100,000 in the year 2014. The inflation rate since the year 2000 has always been between 0.8% and 3.4%. We're going to use the rate of 2% in this example. Keep in mind that if you ever want to know the current inflation rate, you can always google it to get an accurate number. Your money can buy you various things, but since you don't have a direct need for it at that time, you just let it sit in your bank. You don't touch it until this year (2019 as of the time of this writing). With inflation running at 2% in this example, that would be a loss via devaluation of $2,000 per year. There are 5 years between 2014 and 2019, which equals a $10,000 loss! This means that your $100,000, in reality, is $90,000 in the year 2019. After inflation runs its course, your net result is a loss of money. That is why I say the stakes are higher nowadays as opposed to years ago, when it comes to the topic of saving.

140

If you're wondering what the numbers look like in this scenario, they are as follows. The original $100,000 multiply by the annual 2% inflation rate (or 0.02), which gives us a $2,000 loss per year due to inflation. Multiplying that $2,000 by 5, since it has been 5 years since you put the money in there, equals $10,000. You then minus this total loss of inflation from your original $100,000, which gets you the net result of losing money, i.e., $90,000. You might be asking, "But I earn interest when it's in my checking or savings account." That is true, but the rates are not what they used to be. The average interest rate on a savings account as of this writing is 0.06%. This rate on the $100,000 would give you $100,300 by way of multiplying the $100,000 by 0.06%, by 5 years. We now minus the necessary evil of inflation, which is $10,000. This gives us $90,300. This leaves your net loss of purchasing power at $9,700. This example is just over 5 years. What if the period is longer? Also, what if the money amount is larger? Under this model, making more money also means losing more money.

The only way to avoid this is to have your money in places that give you annual returns that exceed or at least match the rate of inflation. This leads to another issue though. If I put my money in something like that, what do I do if I need cash the same day? A lot of the things mentioned later will take 3 to 5 days to get the money out. I can't wait that long! So, where does that leave the concept of savings? Do I keep my money in the bank, so I have quick access to it while it gets eaten up by inflation? Or, do I put my money in an investment savings vehicle like an ETF when it's keeping up with inflation, but it takes longer to get it when I need it? This is the yardstick you measure a savings method by. How fast you can access the funds vs. its ability to keep up with the rate of inflation. I'm happy to say nothing is stopping you from doing both and it's best if you do.

The Multi-Savings Approach

The best way to deal with the problem is to have multiple savings approaches. Don't worry; I would never recommend doing all of these at once as that would be confusing. The key is to do these sequentially. Once your money fully funds one, that savings is complete, and you move on to the next one. This is what I call the immediate cash savings, bank savings, and inflation savings. I'll now go into what each of these is.

Immediate cash savings

As we covered before, things happen. Plumbing problems occur. The washer goes out. The brakes on your car need to be replaced. Sometimes, what comes up is more immediate. Here is the place where you can get $$$ from and address the issue right away. The first savings that should be done right away is to have 6 months to a year's worth of living expenses saved up in cash. It may also be practical to calculate the cost of a safe (to store your $$$) in there if you don't have one already. Not only is this type of savings immediate, but technically, it is the safest one. It's not tied to banks or society in general; hence, when you need it, it's right there.

While it may be tempting to start with the bank savings or inflation savings, this really should be the first one you establish. Write down all of the expenses that you have that are needed. This means these expenses are the minimum standard to operate in today's society. An example would be your mortgage/rent and internet bill, but it would not be your gym membership. Add them all together to get a monthly figure. Multiply that figure by 6 and that will give you the minimum savings number you should have in cash available. Ideally, if you can have a year of savings, that's even better. Beyond a year is where the cons start outweighing the pros when it comes to this method. Inflation isn't going anywhere, and when savings extend beyond a year, that's when it's time to seek vehicles that can offset it.

Bank Savings

Once your cash savings are set up, here is an appropriate next step. The meager interest banks pay these days are usually not of much use. The purpose of bank savings is more so a convenience thing as when somethings do come up, you may have to handle it electronically. That's not to say that banking with a bank that has the highest interest you can find is a bad idea. Just don't compromise other things you choose banks for, like how much the monthly fees are, and how many of them there are just because they pay a little higher interest than others. There's a reason inflation savings and bank savings are 2 different things nowadays. More money often means higher spending and expenses. Due to this, a good practice is to have 10% of your annual income in your bank savings. So, if you make $50,000 a year, $5,000 of bank savings is good to have in the bank. This should be the next phase of your overall savings after your immediate cash savings. Once this has been achieved, it's time to move into the inflation savings.

Inflation Savings

The goal here is to pick an investment vehicle that gives you an annual return of at least the rate of inflation, effectively keeping your money's value with the pace of inflation. As mentioned before, you can always find out the exact rate, but as a common practice, I use 2% as the going rate. There are many investment vehicles that can serve as savings based on the reason we've already laid out. A few inflation savings examples are: Buying precious metals like gold and silver, purchasing bonds that pay fixed rates (which offset inflation), 401k accounts, solo 401k plans, Roth 401K plans, certificates of deposits (the ones offering yields higher than 2%), ETFs, Roth IRAs, traditional IRAs, SEP IRAs. What they all have in common is that they can rise in value faster than the annual rate of inflation.

Like everything, they all have their shortcomings and advantages. To go into those would be a book in itself. The point in mentioning them here is to bring awareness to them. There is nothing wrong with having more than one inflation savings, as long as the previous two are set up. I would caution against over expanding, though. The purpose here is just savings. That's why one or two of these should suffice. You also want to be familiar with or at least understand how what you are putting your money into works. If you want to put money into more than 2 of these, list the ones outside of the one you like the most as investments and not savings. Some things to consider when picking one are how do taxes impact your money and whether there are any fees associated with them.

When you think about it, savings are a very defensive financial activity. Setting up your savings like this gives you 3 lines of defense: the immediate cash savings being the tool you need immediately on the field to fix something, the bank savings being the fort around you, and the inflation savings being a wall that keeps getting built up to protect you from the growing bullet sizes of inflation. Each savings type carries confidence with it that gives you a sense of security. Is that not what playing defensive is all about? Security?

Quick Note on savings: The methods of savings listed are the ones that are the most robotic. Putting this another way, they are the savings that have no emotional influence. While these dynamics won't change regardless of what's going on, there is another type of savings. When was the last time you saved for a vacation? What about saving up money to pay off your car in full? How about saving a lot of money specifically for a particular type of investment or even start a business? Anytime you are budgeting cash for something that you will get in the future (over a month), this is saving. This is to be noted as we will go deep into the type of savings in Chapter 9.

Investments

We work hard for our money. We save some of it realizing we may need it down the line. Something is missing, though. What could it be? All of a sudden, a bell starts to ring in our heads. In a true partnership, we should both be working, right? I shouldn't be doing all the work! That means my money should be working for me too! Welcome to the world of investing. Most people, when they hear this word, think of the stock market or real estate. It's true; these are forms of investing. Investing is more than just putting money into getting more money. At its root, an investment is the spending of money on something that will give you a return. That doesn't have to be a stock or real estate. The return also does not have to be measured in money directly. For instance, a person gets a job at a warehouse, and they buy more comfortable shoes to help them at work. This is an investment for themselves because they are getting a return in the form of less effort and feeling better. These 2 factors could lead to more money because they can now work more overtime. It could also not result in more overtime. Regardless, it's an investment in both cases. An investment can give you a return in how you feel, in cashflow, in leads for your business, in referrals, etc. The point is that the money you spend gets you a return. With that picture being painted, all investments fall into 2 arenas: Direct and indirect.

Direct Investments

These are the stereotypical things you hear about when it comes to investing. Making money from the stock market. Making money from real estate. Buying gold when it's low and selling when it's high. Here is where your assets are. Assets are the exact opposite of liabilities in the expense section. An asset puts money in your pocket. What kind of money and how often is up to you. Direct investments boil down to expecting one of these 3 things:

1.   Cashflow from the investment

2.   Capital gains based on the appreciation of the asset

3.   Both 1 and 2

You must take the time to educate yourself on both the art and science of direct investing. Not doing so can turn investments that have the potential to be assets into liabilities. Yes, this means you can lose money. It's often not even the investment per se that is risky, but rather the inexperience of the investor. Let's take a look at 2 people who are investing in a stock. One has taken courses on investing, and the other has not. Person A who has no education on investing buys stock in the said company. Person B who has the education waits to buy. The share price drops. Person A gets a little nervous. Person B finally decides to buy some shares. The price drops further. Person A panics! With the fear of losing their money, they sell their shares and accept the loss. Person B looks at the earnings reports of the said company and matches it up to the company industry. They come to the conclusion that this is part of a 5-year cycle where they face temporary delays. They then look at information from the past 15 years and sees this same pattern. The company always rebounds. More importantly, Person B remembers that it is the holidays, and people are pulling money out of the stock market to buy gifts. Person B buys more shares. A few months later, the share prices are 25% higher than it was when both bought. Person A is scratching their head, thinking WTF? Person B has made a capital gain of 25%, and they could sell or hold as the share price keeps rising. What was the risk factor in that scenario? The stock, the market, Person A or Person B. It was Person A since they lacked education and control over themselves.

I know you were probably expecting some complicated formula, but it is that simple. One must have the education and control over themselves to benefit here. Direct investments are also things that you spend money on that you do so with the expectation of making more money in the very near future. With me making money from my phone via apps, if I got another phone with a better data plan or if the phone was faster, this would be a direct investment too. Also, keep in mind that if you are in debt, and you are paying more than the minimum amount on that debt, the difference between the minimum amount on that debt and what you pay is also an investment. This is the case because it can cause the debt to be paid off quicker. Once paid off, the cashflow that was going to the debt is now going back into your budget. We can't forget about the other form of investing though, indirect investing.

Indirect investing

This is the more forgotten of the 2. Person B, in the above scenario, clearly invested in their education before actually investing in a direct method. Investing in education can be a form of indirect investing. It can be indirect because you may not see an immediate payoff. The shoe example of the warehouse worker mentioned before is also an indirect investment. It's having a positive impact on how the worker feels and on the level of effort being put out. They could say the right thing at the right time due to feeling normal instead of saying nothing due to their feet hurting. This could land them an interview for a promotion. They now could have more physical and mental energy once they get home to do more constructive moneymaking activities than watching TV to recuperate from a hard day's work. Do you see the ripple effects just buying some new work shoes can have? It's my view that this form of investing is hugely underestimated and taken for granted. It is here where investing is subtler, and things tend to line up in the background without you even noticing sometimes. Am I saying that indirect investing is better than direct? No, I'm not. Most people who do invest only do so in one of these ways. They are 2 sides of the same coin. You will be more abundant financially if you see this and spend money on both when it comes to investing.

Self-spending

This is the main reason we want money in the first place, right? I would hope that's not the only reason. It should not be denied that a desire to get money for the sole reason of spending it on you is only natural. If you don't, you will feel like a slave. You pay your expenses, save your money to ensure it's not devalued, and you're investing money, so you can get more of it. What's the point of all that if you can't enjoy some of it? For those of you with families, spending money on them counts as spending money here too. Why is that, you say? When money is spent on your spouse, son, daughter, etc., how do you feel? Most likely, you feel good or have a sense of accomplishment. Wait, is that not the feeling you get when you spend money on yourself? By family, I mean your immediate family that is in your care, and that you are responsible for on a consistent basis. Not when your sister or brother from another state asks you for $50 randomly. So, what are the things you spend on yourself? It looks like we're going to have some fun with this!

I am sure you've pictured yourself in some of those clothes that you walked by when you were window shopping. At some point, you take the window out of shopping and bam! You've got yourself a wardrobe upgrade. Let's not limit ourselves to just clothes. What about when I want to go to the movies with my friends? That money has to come out of somewhere. I haven't even mentioned dating! What about that massage I get done every month? Yes, I have food listed as an expense, but sometimes, I go over when I want to eat out more that month. Where does that money come from? The hair on my head grows, and I want it shaped to fit my tastes. Oh yeah, that cost money. The trend here is apparent. This part of the budget can be defined as anything you spend money on involving yourself, and it makes you feel good! Trust me; this is much needed. If you didn't spend some of that hard-earned $$$ on yourself now and then, you would have jumped off the roof a long time ago.

Business

This budgeting section won't be applicable if you don't have a business. This is also not for those that have a big company with its own accounts. This is for the self-employed person. From an emotional perspective, the business budget is a combination of all of the budgeting categories. A business has its own investments, money spent that make it look more appealing (self), its own expenses and donations that are often tax-deductible, and savings. Anytime you spend money on these, and it falls under business, it should come from here. In the next chapter, we'll tackle how a certain percentage of your income should go here by default. For now, be aware that this place exists if you are self-employed.

Donations

Like we covered in Chapter 3, we all have causes that we support or are sympathetic towards. It's also important to bring up that donations don't have to strictly be money given to a nonprofit, but rather money that is given in a general way. In a few days, my sister's birthday is coming up, and I will be buying her present tomorrow. The money for her present is coming out of my donation budget. Many people tend to give spontaneously. Since this chapter is about budgeting, it's best to plan for the spending of this. The easiest way to do this is by donating a percentage of your monthly income. It could be 1% or 10%. The key is to take the spontaneity out of it so that it is planned. That doesn't mean the amount has to change in a lot of cases. You may find yourself giving 3% or 5% of your take-home income randomly every 3 months, when a steady 1% donation every month would be better for you and what you are supporting. The organization you're giving to sees the pattern of steady cashflow and can begin making plans for the money and you.

As you may remember, this increases your unorthodox income. I said it once, and I'll repeat it here. For this to happen, you should be giving for the sake of giving and not seeking something in return. Is cash running low? There are other ways to contribute like your time. Here, you want to treat time as a currency, just like money. I'll give a personal example to show you what I mean. I currently have my donations every month, set to 3% of my income. In April, I did a lot of volunteering for the BVSTX. That month, I didn't pay any donations. Why not, you say? I didn't because of the amount of volunteering I did. I came up with an hourly average I would be making if I was doing something else with that time to generate money. It was an average of all my streams of money which came out to be $20 per hour. For every hour I was volunteering, I subtracted $20 from the amount I would pay in donations. This is what I call paying via time. In the end, the time canceled out the money, and that's why I didn't pay any money on donations that month. If the time I spend outweighs the donation budget, the excessive money value of the hours is added to the budget category of my choosing (self, investments, expenses, savings, or business). This will only work if my income is mostly orthodox (steady). If it is more so unorthodox (unsteady), well, there's no need for me to balance the equation. Like I said before, the universe has a way of rebalancing through unorthodox income.

Banking

I sincerely don't think it is possible anymore in today's time to operate in society without banking. If it is, it would certainly be inconvenient. We open bank accounts for various reasons, or at least we should. These are the reasons that should determine what kind of account we start, and what banks we give our business to, since they all have their advantages and drawbacks. We shouldn't open bank accounts simply as a place to receive a direct deposit or just to hold our money. Is the monthly fee that they are charging worth the things that you value when it comes to banking? Do you hate overdraft fees, and this bank doesn't have them? Would you prefer to get charged the overdraft fee than deal with the embarrassment of a debit card decline? Does the bank charge for cashing checks? What interest do they pay on savings accounts? What are the terms of having a savings account? Does the bank have activity standards that need to be met each month, otherwise more fees are triggered? Are there a lot of these banks so that you can withdraw money without fees?

The above army of questions are here for a reason. If banking is a needed expense nowadays, you better get your values worth! At the very least, do they offer significantly better services than these online fee-free banks? Yes, there is such a thing. Simple banking and Moven are 2 examples. Since you work hard for your money, you deserve the best quality and best-priced banking services you can get. Don't short yourself here. It can cost you $$$.

A question that we've all most likely asked ourselves at some point is whether we should have more than one bank account. There are potential pros and cons. Having a single bank account will give you less to keep track of in general. All transactions go through one location. This can be, to some degree, mentally freeing. It can also be cheaper since there will be only one account fee (or none if using an online free one).

On the other side of the coin, having multiple bank accounts can be considered safer since we're in the age where fraud and identity theft is relatively common. These are all variables to think about. What is often not valued is how having one or multiple bank accounts affects the areas of finance. A habit that must be developed for financial success, on a big scale, is the ability to categorize transactions on your financial statement. You can do this on a mundane level. For example, when you go to buy groceries, you may classify this as "food" on your financial statement. The problem is, many people just do this in their heads! They aren't taking advantage of the time period we're in.

Back in the old days, people would write everything down with pen and paper. It was done to ensure money wasn't slipping through the cracks. This time around, there are tools at your disposal that can categorize your transactions. It may seem of little importance now, but you'll see the full significance of this later down the line. For now, you can categorize your statement in the areas of finances that have been covered. This can be done using popular money management apps like the Mint budgeting app or the Prism app, which links to your bank account and allows you to make categories for your spending.

This is relatively simple for someone with just one bank account. Just link that one account and you're good to go. What about those with multiple accounts? Does it get much trickier? Not if you do it the right way. I have 5 bank accounts, and it is still easy for me to do. You just need to have the proper structure for your accounts in place. It starts with you assigning a certain area of finance to a particular bank account. This can be done in a few ways. You want to have a bank account that serves as the central bank for your finances. Every transaction that you do goes through this bank. This includes your streams of income. The easiest way to do this is to link your payment methods with this bank account via account and routing number. Even if you make money in another account, the transaction needs to show up in the central bank somehow. I have payments that go to my PayPal account, but at the end of the week, that amount is transferred to my central bank. That way, the transaction shows up there.

Your central bank should be used only for receiving income, savings, and donations. The exception to this is if you just want to use one bank account. Next, decide what financial areas the other bank accounts will be used for. This can be as convoluted or as simple as you want. You can have 10 accounts for one financial area, or you can have just one. You can also have one bank account used for multiple areas. I would recommend one of these 2 setups. Your central bank and 2 other bank accounts. One bank for the 2 areas that are the most important to you, and the other for the remaining area. If you have a business, set up another separate account just for that. The second way is to have your central bank and 4 other banks for each area. One for self-spending, investments, expenses, and business (omit this if you don't have one).

If you have credit cards, categorize them in terms of the financial areas. Whichever one they fall under, use that area's bank account to deal with that credit card. Regardless of which way you choose, link them all to your central bank. Once you decide to spend money on something, transfer the funds to the account that you've assigned for that financial area. If it is a reoccurring expense, make sure the money in your bank account(s) always equals or exceeds your reoccurring expenses for that account. For instance, I know how much I spend on my phone bill, car note, and house expenses each month. These are linked to my expenses account. I make sure my balance is always higher than these expenses combined. Another example is my Netflix subscription. It is linked to my self-spending account, and I make sure the balance is always higher than the cost of the subscription. This can be done via minimum balances and auto transfers from your central bank, or you can do it manually. It's all up to you.

Once this is done, link an app or service like Mint or Prism to your central bank, or, use a strategic management bank like Simple banking as your central bank. Every time you withdraw or transfer money to another account, categorize that transaction in the area it's going to. This allows you to have the accounting benefits of having just one bank and the benefits of multiple banks at the same time!

"So, what banks should I choose?" That decision will always be yours. I recommend using a combination of online banks and physical banks. That way, you don't have a butt load of money banking fees, but you can also put cash in your accounts when you need to. My banking setup is the following: I use Simple Bank as my central bank, PayPal for business, Chase for investments, Chime Bank for self-spending, and BB&T for expenses (bills). That's 3 online banks (which are free) and 2 physical banks which have small monthly fees. Since I use Simple as my central bank, I don't need to use an app like Mint to categorize my transactions. I do that via Simple's goal management system.

Should My Central Bank be Online or Physical?

Like everything in the financial world, there are pros and cons to both. The biggest advantage to a physical location is that it will allow you to deposit cash and checks to your main financial hub conveniently. You can also physically talk to a banker about anything you need. The biggest con is the physicality of a bank location requires them to increase overhead for the said banking institution. This causes many of them to charge various fees like overdraft and monthly fees. Keep in mind that many physical banks have requirements that can be met that will result in reduced or eliminated fees. When compared to their online counterparts that don't have these fees or requirements, they can seem annoying to some people. Because of a physical bank's overhead, their interest rates on checking and more importantly, savings accounts are usually a joke. If you don't believe me, google the savings interest rates of popular banks like Capital One, Citibank and Chase. With inflation running at an average of 2%, you will be losing money with your savings here. You could always use another account for your savings other than your central bank, but this will become inconvenient. The best savings setup is for your central bank to have a savings account and have automatic transfers to that account from your primary checking. Is the convenience of the pros of a physical bank worth the cons of it? That's something to think about.

Now, let's cover the pros of an online central bank. Since the bank is online, they don't have the overhead of having to run physical branches. This allows them to pay higher interest rates in general, but more so on savings. It's not hard to find an online bank that offers an interest rate equal to or even higher than inflation. With this being the case, it's a no brainer to set up your savings here and have automatic transfers from your checking to your savings. Since your savings will have a better interest rate, you won't be losing ground to inflation.

If the interest rate is higher, you could even make a little money. The biggest con here though is when you want to deposit cash, you'll have to use another account and transfer it to your central bank for accounting purposes. This could take a few days which could be inconvenient to some. You also can't physically talk to someone when you need something taken care of.

So, which one offers the pros that you value the most and the cons that you can put up with? That's the question to ask yourself at the end of the day. As mentioned before, Simple is my central bank, and it has a 2.02% savings interest rate at the time of writing this book. That's about equal to inflation. There are other online banks with higher interest rates, but I like Simple's ability to make goals and categories. For me, that has a higher value than a higher interest rate. I'd be lying if I didn't say that it is a little inconvenient when I have cash to deposit that I have to go through Chase or BB&T, and then transfer it to Simple. Since I make most of my money online nowadays though, this rarely comes up anymore. It all comes down to what you want and what you're willing to put up with.

Building and managing credit

A financial blueprint wouldn't be fully complete without touching on the topic of credit. Webster's dictionary defines credit as "the ability of a customer to obtain goods or services before payment, based on the trust that payment will be made in the future." In today's society, to have this privilege, the said financial intuition will charge you an amount of interest. The determining factor on what interest rate you get (if you even get approved) is your credit score. Developing a good credit score can assist you when you want to finance things that you don't want to buy in full right now. These 5 things impact your credit score.

1. Your credit history

2. Your credit utilization rate

3. The amount of on-time payments

4. The mix of the lines of credit you have available

5. The total amount of inquiries on your report

Seeing how there are full books on the subject of credit, I won't bore you with the details of it here. Should you want to know more about it, a quick google search of the things mentioned above will provide the full picture you need. If you are looking to establish credit, meaning you have a nonexistent credit score, doing the following steps will help you toward obtaining a good credit score. The first thing you should do to develop a score is to go to one of your physical banks and get what's known as a secured credit card. This means that you put down a set amount, usually around a few hundred dollars, and in return, they give you a credit card with your deposit that you have given them as collateral against the credit card. If you don't pay off your credit card, they hold your deposit, so they can pay off the credit card. Putting down between $200 to $500 is enough to get you started. This will give you a $200 to $500 credit limit for the credit card. It is the best and easiest way for a bank to accept you as a first-time credit card applicant.

Do not go crazy buying things that you can't afford! Treat it just like you treat cash. Use it to pay for things that you would normally pay with cash. Just use this card instead, and pay off the balance in full with the cash you were going to use to buy the things at the end of every month (or before your credit card due date). It's a myth that you have to pay interest on a credit card for it to raise your score. As long as you pay it off every month, you are building credit. There is no need to pay any interest. Doing this for about 6 months will get the ball rolling on establishing your credit history. After you've successfully done this, you should be able to apply for an unsecured credit card. Repeat the same thing you did with the secured card for another 6 months. You should have a decent credit history now and can apply for a charge card. These are the cards that offer rewards and points that you can use in a variety of ways. At this point, you should have a pretty good credit score. If your credit score is less than stellar, consider using a reputable credit repair service, and while they do their magic, try and get the unsecured credit card going. I would say this is something everyone should do if you don't have any credit history, or if you have a poor credit score. Regardless of whether you choose to use credit or not, it is good to have in your inventory should you ever need it. Just handle it responsibly!

Quick note on credit: For the past 100 years or so, it has been the new normal to simply finance things "just because." It is these types of irrational decisions that cause people's earnings to spending ratio to get out of whack in the first place. Before doing this, make sure you see the impact that said activity would have on your budget, both in the short and long term. It may be better just to save up the cash. Don't just finance something because that's just what people do. Have your own reason and look at the full picture. It's this ability that separates the financially savvy person from the average Joe or Jane.

CHAPTER 8.

THE BUDGET FOR SUCCESS:

A WAY TO ENSURE YOU KEEP MOVING FORWARD

"A budget is telling your money where to go instead of wondering where it went."

—Dave Ramsey, Professional real estate and stock market investor

---

A fitting quote seeing how we are about to dive into the nuts and bolts of how to make a successful budget. We've covered the areas of a budget, but how does one move forward financially? Do they just work hard? If that was true, you could hit the ground running after just reading the income chapters. Unfortunately, we don't have to look far to see examples of people who are making money and still have financial problems. Hold on! I thought the popular thought was if I make more money, my issues will be over. While that's a common assumption, have we ever thought of who said that? That's assuming anyone said it at all. Regardless if it was said and popularized or if we come to that conclusion, we have to accept the fact that there is more to it than that. If you doubt me, look at all the people who won the lottery and ended up back where they started or worse in a few years. On the flip, there's a handful of them that manage to keep that money and do well. What gives? What are they doing that the others didn't do? The answers are in the previous chapter. A plan for spending money on yourself, investments, expenses, savings, your business, and donations are all part of the dynamics of financial success. I like to call it the "cycle of money." The lack of funds focused in the right way on one or more of the areas (excluding business if you don't have one) is the cause of financial failure.

How Ignoring these Causes Failure

I doubt I have to tell you the repercussions of not paying your bills and expenses. When you wake up and your car is being towed like Denzel Washington in the movie John Q, you see the importance of paying that car note. If you don't pay your expenses, it has a ripple effect in your life. Don't pay house expenses; you have to go without them. This increases stress on you, which can affect how you feel, which in turn can affect your money. Let's say you can squeeze by without that car. The situation won't end without taking a ding on your credit rating, making it that much harder to buy other things in the future. We're not even going to go into if the debt gets sent to collection. Just as it was demonstrated in Chapter 6, expenses are part of the society we live and neglecting them has both in the moment and future repercussions.

Just like expenses, having savings is something we know we have to take care of. Life happens, and you need to be ready for it. What if something happens where you need money? You now have to go generate the funds to take care of the issue. The timing couldn't be worse. Your attention should be on leveraging an opportunity for you to learn something or make more money, but instead, it has to go to making money to fix a problem a savings account could have fixed. For example, let's say there's a fitness boot camp you signed up for, but since your transmission is out, you're missing out on a program you paid (or are paying) for until it's fixed. How do you feel when you have a savings account with money in it? Safe to say you feel good, right? A feeling of knowing you're ok if life happens. If we dig deeper though, the good feeling is coming from being in control. If life does happen, you can move things around to stay in control. When we don't have money to deal with financial problems that come up, it often makes us feel like we are not in control of our financial lives. Since money is so integrated into our everyday life, that's a horrible feeling to have. Having savings gives a lot of people the confidence to move forward with other ways of making money that might otherwise be risky, because they know they have savings if stuff hits the fan. Whether we realize it or not, that savings has a direct and subtle impact on us.

Many of us don't get ahead because we don't have our money bringing us something in return. We put in work and spend some on ourselves, bills, and save some of it. Then, we repeat the cycle. This is a plan to stagnate. If we don't spend any money on investments, we have nothing coming our way. Spending money on investments lays the grounds for something to come your way. That something can be more money, or it can be an opportunity to make you more money. It could be ways to reduce your expenses. There are plenty more examples that show how a lack of spending on this is an issue in terms of progressing financially. As pointed out in Chapter 7, the 2 types of investments, i.e., direct and indirect, should BOTH be given attention. What would it look like if you blew all your money in the stock market without investing in financial education first? Investing is the subtlest among the 6 areas of finance because if you ignore spending money on investments, your life can still seem fine with no problems. Eventually, it will click that your standard of living is peaking. Then you wonder how you can stop this from happening.

Easily having the most direct impact, neglecting yourself or the "self spending" area when it comes to money affects you in more ways than I could list here. They all have this common theme, though. If you are putting in the work for money, but don't spend any on yourself, you start to feel like a slave. People that ignore this area usually come down with seemingly random illnesses. If you look at their situations, they are not random. If you abuse yourself by not rewarding yourself for the work you put in, it shows up negatively in your health in various ways. Even if you don't get sick, you'll find it affects how you are socially, energetically, etc. That can have adverse effects on those around you too. How does your spouse feel when you're feeling bad? How do they feel when you are simply not feeling good? Basically, it affects the quality of life for the worse. What's the point of living life if you're not going to live life?

I discussed how donations and businesses contribute to a budget in Chapter 7, so I won't mention it here. The point to drive home though is that there are only 2 directions you can go financially--forward or backward. Neglecting one or more of the 6 financial areas (5 if you don't have a business) is what causes you to move backward. Likewise, giving all of these areas attention and money will ensure that you keep moving forward. Of course, that's assuming you are either making the amount of money you want to make, or your income is increasing to reach that amount in the future. If this is not the case, a level of focus needs to be given to the income chapters of this book so that you can strengthen your financial arms and legs. So, how do you budget with these 6 areas in a way that ensures you are moving forward financially?

Up until this point, there has been a balance between generalizing and detail. For this section, we have to tilt the glass closer to the detailed. It may seem tedious at first, but once you get a feel for it, it can be fun. The following is a formula that can be used to budget, covering the 6 (5 if you don't have a business) main areas that I mention in the budget phase of this book. Keep in mind that the separate business area is for those that are self-employed or have their own business that is not a separate entity. If for example, you have an LLC, you wouldn't want to use this hybrid budgeting system. Instead, you would keep your personal finances and your LLC separate, so it makes accounting easier. A business that is separate from yourself has its own spending on expenses, investments, savings, self (employee appreciation, corporate parties, employee of the month rewards, etc.) and donation to worthy causes that are tax-deductible. If this is being done for a business separately, there should still be a business section. Just rename it to taxes and treat the tax section like the business section for the hybrid system. This process can be set up using budgeting software like Excel or done literally by hand. For illustration purposes, it will be shown to you by hand. You will find that all budgets are either watered down or more detailed versions of what you will see. It is because the 6 areas of a successful budget are universal, undeviating, and objective. The only thing that varies between 2 successful budgets is the degree of details these 6 areas are given. I call this budget: The cycle of $$$ success.

Draw a circle of $$$ and the formula in the middle. This part is optional, but it adds flavor to an otherwise dull topic. Feel free to skip this step if you want. We're going to budget for a month and use a $4,000 monthly income in this example.

Step 1: Write the word "Income" and an = sign. Then write down your monthly income. For this example, it is $4,000.

Step 2: In a true budget, donations/tithes need to be a priority. The only sensible way this can be achieved is to plan for and spend money here first before anything else, with the exception being food. This means before you look at the other areas, this area needs to be addressed. Come up with a percentage of your income that you will give to donations. How much is up to you, but I've found that a good minimum is 3%. If you can't give at least 3% of your income to worthy causes, then it's time to focus on increasing income (Phase 2). Once you come up with the percentage, multiply your income by that percentage. For this example, we will use a minimum of 3%: $4,000 x 0.03 = $120. This gives us $120 to spend on donations. Write down the amount that will be paid to donations. The equation used here is Income X Donation percentage = Amount spent on donations.

Step 3: Subtract the amount you will spend on donations from your income. This would be $4,000 - $120 = $3,880. Write down the new number. This is how donations/tithes are prioritized. The equation used here is Income - Amount spent on donations = Leftover income. The percentage you spend is deducted from your total income before the other areas are in the equation. Steps 4, 5, and 6 are for people with businesses. Skip these steps if you don't have a business.

Step 4: Come up with a percentage that will go towards your business. When doing this, take how much you pay in taxes into consideration. This is the place where things you spend on business will come from and likewise, most of those are tax-deductible. I've found that a good number is 25%.

Step 5: Take your income with donations out and multiply it by your business percentage. Here, it will be $3,880 x 0.25 = $970. It is fine to round up or down. The equation here is Leftover income x Business percentage = Money spent on business. This acts as a self-cleaning system, so you won't get drummed at the end of the year with a huge tax bill. I'm not saying that a bill won't be there. This percentage is to be used if you are just starting. After your first year, you should have a better feel as to what this percentage should be.

Step 6: Subtract the business number from the current income: $3,880 - $970 = $2,910. The equation in this step is: Leftover income - Money spent on business = New leftover income.

Step 7: Write down the other 4 areas in a vertical line. Make sure the 2 areas that you are going to give the most attention to are first.

Step 8: Look at your financial statement over the past few months (or last month) and come up with a total of how much your monthly expenses are. These are the recurring type of expenses covered before (food, rent, car note, etc.). Note that these should be the expenses needed for everyday life and not luxury. For our example, there is a car note, food expenses, rent, internet, utilities, cell phone, and car insurance. This totals $1,400 in our example.

Step 9: Multiply your monthly expense number by 10%. Here, this would be $1,400 x 0.10 which is $140. Add this number to your monthly expenses. If putting individual things in your budget, call this Misc. Expenses. The equation is Expenses (added together) x 10% = Misc. Expenses. This is done to account for the non-reoccurring expenses that just happen to some degree. It's time for an oil change, etc. I find that these expenses tend to increase as our standard of living expands. It usually runs around 5 to 10% of your overall expenses, which is why we used the number of 10% here. If nothing comes up during this budget period for this money, you can give it to one of the other 3 categories left; preferably the one that needs the most work. This brings the total money to be spent on expenses to $1,540.

Step 10: The following has to be done to find out what percentage of your income is going towards expenses. Take the current income (the number you came up with in step 6 if you have a business, step 3 if you don't) and subtract your monthly expense total from it: $2,910 - $1,540 = $1,370. Next, divide that number by your current income (same number): $1,370 ÷ $2,910= 0.4707. Multiply this number by 100: 0.4707 X 100 = 47.079. Round this number up or down and subtract it from 100. 100 - 47 = 53. Slap a percentage on that, and you have the percentage you pay in expenses.

Step 11: It's time for savings! If you have not reached having 6 months to a year's worth of cash, this should be the first priority here. For this example, they have not reached 6 months. In fact, they don't have a savings! Take your expenses and cut them in half: $1,540 ÷ 2 = $770. Take this number and do the formula we've been doing, i.e., Income - this number ($770 in this example). Divide that number by your current income. Multiply this number by 100. Round this number up or down and subtract it from 100. $2,910 - $770 = $2,140. $2,140 ÷ $2,910 = 0.7353. 0.7353 x 100 = 73.53. Rounding up, you get 100 - 74 = 26. This will put you on the track to reach 6 months' worth of savings in a year. If you can't do this percentage yet, you have to start somewhere. Just keep this number in the back of your mind as it is the number that will put you on the track in a year's worth of time. If you already have at least 6 months to a year's worth of savings in cash, then there's not as much of a need to put a lot of funds here. The savings vehicles talked about before can start taking place. Just make sure that the money you put toward savings doesn't drop below 5%. Taking the income ($2,910) and multiplying it by the savings percentage (26% or 0.26) will give the example $757 to put towards savings.

Step 12: Decide how much you want to spend on investing! Your expenses have been figured out as well as savings. Pick a percentage to go here out of what's left. For this example, 53% is expenses and 26% is savings. This leaves 21% for the other 2 areas. Let's use 12% for this area. Multiply the current income by the percentage you choose: $2,910 x 0.12 = $349.

Step 13: Decide how much you want to spend on yourself! How much is going on you? Since 9% is what's left, it's going here. Multiply the current income by this percentage: $2,910 X 0.09 = $262.

Income = $4000

Donations = 3% ($120)

Business 25% ($970)

$4000 X 0.03 = $120

4000 – 120 = $3880

$3880 X 0.25 = $970

$3880 – $970 = $2910

Total Monthly Expenses = $1400

$2910 – $1400 = $1510

$1510 ÷ $2910 = 0.5189

0.5189 x 100 =51.89 or 52% (rounded up)

100 - 52 = 48

Total Monthly Expenses % = 48%

$1400 x 0.10 = $140

Misc Expenses = $140 and 10 %

$1400 + $140 = $1540

Total Expenses = $1540 and 53%

Expenses: $1,540 (53%)
Savings: $757 (26%)
Investments: $349 (12%)
Self: $262 (9%)

Step 14: Check yourself! Add all the areas up. They should all add up to the income you started with unless you've done some rounding. Then, it may be off between 0.25 cents and $5. You can do something to make these numbers stand out, so when you check yourself, it's easy to spot them. That's why in this example, they are in bold print. I just look for the financial area words and the numbers next to them, and I add them!

$1,540+$757+$349+$262+$970+$120=$3,998

I know that may seem like a lot, but the key to success here is repetition. The more you do it, the easier it will get. If you put your mind to it, you'll be able to do it by hand (with a calculator) in a short time frame. One month, I was so busy that I was literally out most of the day, every day for a while. While I was heading to Mellow Mushroom to eat lunch, I decided I was going to do the budget while inside. It needed to be done for the month, and I had everything I needed to do it. All I needed was paper, a pen/pencil, and the calculator that's inside my phone. I took paper and a pen with me inside. I wrote down part 1 of the process. The waitress took my order, and 20 minutes later, she brought out my pizza. I already had the budget mapped out, and I was setting the numbers up in my bank account. Yes, there are bank accounts out there that let you put your budget into the banking, like Simple Bank and Moven.

That may sound insane to some of you, but I'm able to do this because I've done this formula over 50 times. This is the level you can get to with practice, and when it comes to budgeting, there is no better practice than the real thing. This can be used to map out any interval of time throughout the year, e.g., a week, a month, a quarter, or a year. If you want to get practice in, a great way is to do it weekly until you get comfortable with it and can do it with ease. From there, move it to when you want. I find that a month is a reasonable interval to do it. I also have to mention that in the example, all the numbers were rounded up which makes the numbers slightly off. It's not enough to make a big difference, though. It's up to you how precise or general you want it to get. Feel free to do the calculations without rounding up using the exact numbers. Once income starts getting above $10,000, that's when it may be in your best interest to do the precise numbers since the numbers are bigger.

Keep in mind that this is how the budget formula works in a step-by-step fashion. That doesn't mean you spend your money in this order. You can, but that's not what's important here. This method gives you an outline to allocate and prioritize these areas of finances to get you success. This is why you NEVER want any of these areas to fall below 5% (Donations is the exception). As shown in the example, it's a tight budget, but as long as you stick to it, you will keep moving forward financially, because money is being spent in every area. When an area has less than 5% of your earned funds spent in it, the other areas are moving faster, and it's getting left behind. This leads to you emotionally undervaluing it, which means it can't fulfill its purpose. Eventually, it will be the cause of you moving backward or becoming stagnant. If areas are so heavy that they are causing other areas to go under 5%, then it's time to focus on increasing your income at a fast rate.

This formula is also a great starting place and can even be used in more advanced budgeting. It doesn't necessarily have to replace how you budget as that decision is a personal one. I will say that you should ask yourself this question, "Does this formula seem somewhat familiar?" If it does, then that's a good sign your current method of budgeting contains the fundamentals of a budget. The fundamentals being donations, business (for some), expenses, investments, self, and savings. If what was shown in the example seemed unfamiliar or like a foreign language, it may be a sign that this formula would do you better than your current method. The critical points in a budget should do the following things.

1. Cover the 5/6 areas of a successful budget.

2. Include the percentages of those areas in it.

3. Show where you are strong at and where you need improvement.

Many budgets may cover 1 and 3, but 2 is just as relevant and is often missing. As you will find out in the next phases of this book, the percentage of money you spend on these areas play a role in your ability to make more money.

Assignment 1

If you feel this formula is better than your current way of budgeting, do the formula weekly for the next 2 months. This will build that repetition you need to have it become part of your financial being. In doing so, the 5/6 areas and the concept of their percentages will become second nature to you. From there, continue doing it weekly or switch to monthly. If you feel your current way of budgeting is adequate, go over your budget and categorize each thing in the budget as one of the 5/6 areas. Add all of the numbers up in each area and find out what percentage of your money is going to each area. Even if your budgeting process is already successful, categorizing these 5/6 areas, as well as their percentages, will allow you to gauge where you are, both financially and emotionally. What area do you spend the most money on? What area do you spend the second most money on? For this assignment, don't include the business area or donations. Keep these in mind as they will be brought up in later chapters.

Assignment 2

You have your percentages down, effectively budgeting for every area. This won't mean much if you don't know what goes in each area. On a blank sheet of paper, draw 3 vertical lines with the same distance between each other. If you have a business, draw 4 lines. Towards the top of the page, draw a horizontal line. This should give you 4/5 sections. At the top of the horizontal line, write an area for each section. Those areas being expenses, investments, self, and savings (business too, if present). If you need a section for donations, feel free to add one, but you can also revisit your assignment in Chapter 3 of organizations that you want to support. Next, write down all the things you want or need and categorize them based on these areas. Note that something can be in more than one category. The example of a worker buying new shoes used earlier in this book is a case where they could put those shoes in both the investment area and self-area.

If you have a business, you will find that things in the business section are combinations of 1 or more areas. The only difference is that they are spent on the business and are potentially tax-deductible. When you do put something in the business section, put something next to it to show what it is like in terms of the other areas. It could be a small letter. For example, you purchased a new computer for the business. I would put an "I" next to it since it is an investment for the business. My domain hosting for my website, I would put an "E" next to it for expense. It doesn't matter much for this chapter, but in the next phase, "Spending your money," this will play a decent size role. Ignore this if a business is not in your equation. If your budget is on the computer or if you've done the first assignment, most likely these specific things you're budgeting for are already there. There is no need to repeat this since you've categorized them by the areas.

These assignments will get you familiar with categorizing all things in your budget by these areas. This is vital because budgeting is a plan to spend money here, and spending money fuels different aspects of your emotions, for better and for worse. How so, you ask? That's what the next phase is about. For now, it's time to go into the best strategic money management for you.

What is your ultimate financial goal?

So, we know the basics of budgeting, and we know the breakdown of how we're spending our money. You thought, "I am good to go, right?" By usual standards, yes, you are. However, one thing I have yet to see anywhere is actually taking your personality into consideration when budgeting. "Consider your personality when budgeting! What are you talking about?" These questions may be going through your head. You might even be thinking that phrase is a metaphor for something else. As crazy as it may sound, I literally meant what I said. You might be wondering how is that even possible? That is precisely what the next phase is about. Before we jump into that though, you have to know what you want financially.

Everything we've covered in this book will only be half effective if you do not have what I'm about to mention. You need a financial goal in the way of a number. If you've been keeping tabs, you know that the assignments have been leading up to this. This number represents what you want in terms of time, money and expectations. This was mentioned in Chapter 2, but we didn't attach a figure yet, because it may have seemed out of reach. Now, you know how to increase your income and effectively budget the income you bring in. The number that you choose will seem possible since the methodology of how to get there has been laid out. You still have to put in the work, but you can't build the perfect house without the right tools.

Assignment 3

Review your assignment or list from Chapter 2. It's time to do some research. What is the magic number that will allow you to have or experience all the things on your list regularly? Put a focus on the word "regularly." What number will allow you to live your preferred lifestyle? House, car, vacation, date life, entertainment, donations, helping family and friends, learn what you want with money not being a barrier, etc. These are just some of many things to get you going. If you need inspiration, google "The cost of X." Some prices will start appearing. You may have even done this before, but trust me, this time will be different because you have the system and knowledge of money to make this happen! This number needs to be very personal.

Don't just say, "I want a million dollars a year!" Unless what you want would require a million dollars a year reoccurring. What do you need that money for? A private jet? Are you starting a franchise? Are you getting involved in multi-unit real estate? If some of these are what you want, then that number would make sense. If not, then that's not the number for you. On the same token, don't undershoot it either. This is why research is key. You can even talk to a financial advisor about a financial plan to be comfortable. They can run things by you that you may never have known to be possible at certain income levels. Is it $50,000, $100,000, $500,000, a million? Feel free to take a few days to come up with this number if you need to.

Talk to your friends and family about it. Leave out the pessimistic ones and talk to the encouraging ones. The people that may help you add more things to your initial list! Once you come up with this annual number, divide it by 12, and you have the monthly income you'll need to make each month to reach it! Add both numbers to your original list done in Chapter 2. Either at the top or bottom, write Annual: Your number, Monthly: Your number ÷ 12. You might be wondering what type of income it should be based on Chapter 5. That's jumping ahead of the game. First, you want to make the income goal amount. Once it's made, feel free to repeat this assignment specifying what type of income or combination of incomes you want this number to come by. This doesn't mean you shouldn't be working to make this number through the income types you want, but rather if an opportunity arises to make the target number that you can do, and it's not the income you want, you might want to consider it. As always, that is up to you.

Let the Numbers Push You Forward

Now that you have your goal number, you need to figure out where you stand currently. This can be undervalued at times. You can't map out how to get somewhere until you at least know where you are at. I remember when I had 2 part-time jobs. One was at Amazon before I got promoted to PA, and the other was at Whole Food Market. Both added up to working between 40 to 60 hours a week. I was always tired and burned out, but I felt good about myself since I was putting in so much work. Before then, I only had part-time job positions because they didn't want to give full-time benefits in most cases, with the exception being at Amazon during the holidays when you could get more hours. One day, I decided to do the math and see how much I was making for the year with these 2 jobs. At Whole Foods, I was getting paid $11 an hour, and at Amazon, it was $11.75. When I did the math, it turned out I was making about $31,000 a year. I remember just staring at the calculator for 5 minutes. At that point, I realized that something's not right about this situation. There is no way I could be working this hard and making this amount of money. Only after doing that did my mind start to entertain making a target number, which at the time was $150,000 a year. Once you get your annual income, divide that by 12, and you will have your average monthly income. "How do I get from here to there?" Good question! A better thought is, "How fast do you want to get there?" This determines a large part of how you should approach getting there. Below are the steps to a formula you can use to figure out how to measure and stay on track with reaching your goal in your desired time frame. We will use the following numbers for the example:

Current Monthly Income: $4,000

Desired Annual Income: $150,000

Step 1: Let's say I want to reach an annual goal of $150,000 in 10 years. I divide $150,000 by the number of months in a year, which is 12. That will give me $12,500. This number will be the monthly income you will need to make in order to be making your annual goal.

Step 2: From here, you need to come up with the number of months you want to use to reach your financial goal. You already have this in years, but here, it needs to be converted into months. Simply multiply your time frame in years by 12 and this will give it to you in months, 10 x 12 = 120 months.

Step 3: Next, you need to determine your current monthly income number. You can do this by looking at your most recent financial bank statement. If your funds are more scattered, you may need to look at all of your bank accounts. This is another reason having a central bank is a good idea. It makes accounting much more manageable. We will use $4,000 as an example.

Step 4: Subtract your current monthly income from your desired one: $12,500- $4,000 = $8,500.

Step 5: Divide this number by the number of months you want to use to reach your goal: $8,500 ÷ 120 = $70.83.

In order to reach this goal within 10 years, the person's monthly income needs to increase by $70.83 each month to stay on track to hit the target on time. A good way to use this effectively is to budget using the cycle of money formula covered earlier in the chapter and add this amount to your monthly total each time. You will then have to come up with ways to make this extra amount each month to stay on track. If you come up short one month, you have 2 options: You can keep proceeding as if you hit it. That means that in your next month's budget, you would be adding another $70.83 on top of last month's monthly goal or you can reevaluate either your time frame or your goal. If you genuinely want to get ahead, you'll do the first one. It will keep challenging you to look for ways to increase your income.

It is also important to remember that streams of income may not take off immediately but reap the rewards later. Do you want to do the formula again only to find out that you will be on track or even ahead of the game months later when the streams you put the work in for start making money? If you do choose to reevaluate the goal or time frame, it's best to do it later. Just remember that the problem of not enough money will be a reoccurring theme in your whole life until you get comfortable with raising income. Extending the time frame will only prolong this process. On the flipside, shortening this time frame will speed it up. If at any point, you are ahead of schedule or just want your goal sooner in life, run the formula with a shorter time frame. In my experience, people's income rises slowly when they focus on the wrong type of income for them. If they focus on the right type, they find their income growing at either the rate of their time frame or ahead of schedule. I should mention the fact that these formulas in the book so far are done by hand for illustration purposes. But, they can also be put and integrated into programs like Excel.

You now have a goal and a time frame to reach it in. Now, it's time to fulfill that promise on budgeting for that personality. Before we do that, you have to know what personality you are. Yes, you heard me, right? That is the entire focus of the next chapter.

It may be starting to get old, but I can't help but say yet again congratulations on completing Phase 3. This next phase will feel different. Why will it feel different, you may ask? It will feel different because this phase, more than any other, will take how you feel into the most consideration. It's spending money! If you spend money and feel nothing, I'm tempted to ask if you're a robot or something. When getting our earnings to spending ratio in order, we often focus just on the earnings part and minimize spending. Part of being financially savvy is to know HOW to spend money, not avoid it entirely. Seriously, we hear all the time from those around us that we need to spend more money on this or not spend so much on that. How do they know what's best for us? Since money is an emotional subject, what works for one person may not work for you. So, who are they to tell you how to spend your money? How would they know what's best for you? The truth is, they don't. It must ultimately be done by yourself. Even with this being the case, we often feel uncertain or bad about spending money on certain things. This phase will develop your financial chest, giving you the confidence to spend money on the things that are your emotional strengths and your weaknesses. Go ahead and say it, "Emotional strengths and weaknesses. What do you mean?" Why explain it here when we can jump into the phase?

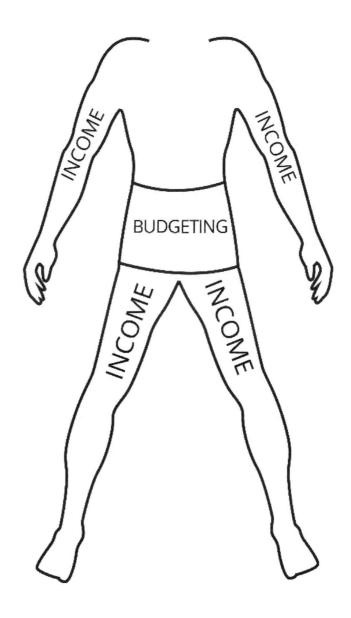

PHASE 4. SPENDING

CHAPTER 9.

THE 6 PERSONALITIES THAT MAKE UP FINANCES

"The key to success is playing to people's strengths."

Blair Singer, a multi-millionaire and author of the sales dogs, the best-selling book and sales personality system.

In his best-selling book, Blair Singer does an amazing job at covering how there are different personality types in sales and how you should tailor your approach based on your personality. That's fantastic but did you know the same applies to finances in general, not just sales? Have you ever felt pressured doing one thing financially and felt great doing something else? Are there particular dynamics of finances that are second nature to you or just come effortlessly to you? On the flip side, are some things just hard? We all have strengths and weaknesses when it comes to money. Yes, our weakness can be improved on, but how do you know if something is a weakness for you? Of course, you will find out eventually through trial and error, but what if there was a way to know what your strengths and weakness were right off the bat? I don't really do what-if scenarios. That's why I'm glad to tell you that there is and this is what this chapter is about. How is this so? It's all in that item people call a financial statement. How you spend your hard-earned money does more than tell a story. It unveils the main character in that story; that story being your life. Remember the 5/6 areas of finances? How much of your money you spend on each area regularly is a direct reflection of your financial personality. Yes, I know that's an eccentric statement. This chapter will make that fluffy like statement real. Each one has a goal style, emotion style, a way of paying their bills, income type, and ability that is best suited for them. The goal, emotional, and bill pay styles will be covered in the next chapter. This chapter will get you familiar with the 6 personas and identifying which one you are. Grab your scuba gear because we're about to go in deep!

Why a financial personality is so important

When I was in high school, I ran cross country and track. In my sophomore year, my coach said that commitment would trump natural talent every day of the week. I always found that statement interesting because I would see people trying so hard and would stay on JV while some people would not work as hard and would be on varsity because they were faster. Whether that statement is true or not, it is ultimately irrelevant. I always thought, why can't you just find something that you're talented at and commit to developing that talent? That was my case, and I was the only sophomore on varsity. Everyone else who was a junior or senior had to run on JV since I was taking the 7th varsity spot on the team.

If only we can apply that thought process to finances. The world of money is enormous, unclear, and full of opportunities. Out of all of that, only some of them, you may have the natural talent for. This means that the understanding of the dynamics of the said financial activity is understood, moderately easy and doing it is not hard for you. It may even be fun! This is the case for everything we've covered in this book. Everyone has a type of income that best fits their personality, a way of managing their emotions, a way of setting financial goals, a way of paying bills, and a way of spending their money. It is why you obtain information on how to do something financially (increase income, set money goals, etc.) and it doesn't work. Often, there is nothing wrong with the information. It just may not fall in your financial personality. It would take a level of hard work and adaptation to do it. Taking what we are naturally talented at and maximizing it is already hard enough. Maybe after we've done and mastered that, looking elsewhere for expansion could be practical. So, what are the 6 personalities that make up the financial world?

The Builder

Things are the result of hard work and long-time consistence. Equipped with his tools (technology, resources, etc.), he sets out to finish his project. He wants a building done at the end of the road. This building has a strong foundation and will still be here long after he has passed on. That means that his descendants will be able to use this building too. This financial building provides a stable place for him to live as well as a roof for other projects he wants to do. Have you ever wanted to do a project, but lacked the resources (money, buildings, assets, etc.)? He does not like to be in this situation. He loves having the building that he lives in and can use to support other things he is interested in.

Since he lives in his building, he doesn't have to make financial commitments just because of money. He can use his time and money to support things that are important to him, whether it brings profits or is for nonprofits. Like any type of building, the value tends to increase over time, and overall cashflow for it rises and falls slowly. He loves this lack of volatility because if something happens, that's not part of the plan, he has plenty of time to make adjustments and react.

Once he builds his 1st building, he realizes that there are benefits to having multiple buildings. He just has to duplicate the fundamentals of what he did for his first building. It's easy. After all, he created the system that allowed for the building to exist in the 1st place. Duplicating it shouldn't be hard. Before he knows it, his love of building systems leads to having many buildings (cashflow) that lay the foundation for a financial empire. This is the dream. To do so, he has to make the plans for the building. It is nothing more than a system to expand while maintaining the structure that's been built up. He can make the plans himself or hire an architect (financial advisor). If he doesn't have the funds to hire one, he can piece together fragments of other systems he sees in society that are working to make his own up. It is this that made him successful in his construction profession initially. Each building of income could be businesses, stocks, bonds, real estate, or anything that brings in constant cashflow once it's up and running. Once he has the plans ready, all that remains is to put in the work!

The builder also has a dual reputation. Not only does he build in the fashion mentioned, but he also builds relationships with others. He is aware that opportunities are directly tied to the quality of your relationships with others. If you have excellent and many relationships, you tend to go far and have more opportunities to make more money. If you have poor or limited relationships, your options are limited. Knowing this, he is always seeking to build upon the relationships he has or forges with others.

Best income source: OP

The best way of dealing with their emotions: Emotional management

The best way of goal setting: Freeflow goals

The best way of paying bills: Bill Autopay

What makes a builder: Investments and savings

It doesn't matter which one has more money in it. If the bulk of the spending in a budget is in investments and savings, this is what makes a builder. He often has a long term goal that he is saving for, while at the same time he spends money on things that will give him a return sooner than the long term goal. He does this naturally because he has a long term plan (saving), and he wants to finance it by spending money on things that will make him more money (investments). This lays the ground for recognizing the cycle of money, and how to use it to his advantage to reach his goals. These cycles could be businesses, stocks, real estate, sales, etc. These people to save and spend money on investing automatically, which makes this a massive strength for getting ahead. All they need is the right information and system, and this can produce a system on autopilot! Money coming in is invested in making more money in the future via total return. Part of that goes to savings and the rest back to investments. Then the cycle repeats! Each time with more money in and coming back! Below are some examples of activities that are both savings and investments that would be in the builder's wheelhouse.

1. Investing in getting a new skill that takes 30 to 90 days to learn but allows you to start making money immediately. Then using the increased income to contribute toward what you're saving for.

2. Having dividends from stocks reinvested via drip (dividend reinvestment program), using them (investment) to acquire more stock(s) that you're using as a savings vehicle.

3. Buying something that produces more money and saving the money that item creates. This MacBook Pro that I'm using to writing this book has made me 1000s of dollars. That money can be saved.

4. Picking a savings account or vehicle that pays interest equal to or higher than inflation and putting money made from your investments here.

The Builder's weakness: Expenses and self-spending

By weaknesses, I mean that they are emotionally weak in these areas. Of course, this can be changed. Since they are emotionally strong in savings and investing, they can get in the bad habit of living in the future. Expenses and spending money on yourself are more in the present than in the future. You pay your expenses, or you'll have immediate problems. You spend money on yourself to emotionally recharge yourself for the next push. The builder can get in a bad habit of neglecting these two and spending money just on investments and savings. Don't neglect these. If you get behind on your expenses, they can compromise your ways of getting funds for your projects, investments, business, etc. There is such a thing as a credit rating. On the same token, the lack of spending on yourself is where the depression comes from. Acknowledge that it is ok to spend money on yourself. Don't feel bad about it. You worked hard, so reward yourself! If you can't enjoy the luxuries of life, what the heck are you here for?

The Builder's Special Ability

This persona has x-ray vision. Ok, not literally, but the builder can see things that most can't see. They see the system behind projects. It comes to them intuitively once they know enough about something. Since they have this ability, they can either duplicate a system they've seen or build their own combining elements of several systems. Creating a system requires one to be categorial, detailed, and hard working. Their love of systems and the ability to build them is how they can be so methodical. They make systems on top of systems, developing a hierarchy, and this allows them to benefit from the concept of compounding. One thing is BUILDING off of another. This, by default, makes them good at scaling projects and numbers like calculating total returns with interest rates and projecting future numbers to see if profit will be made or if there will be a loss of money. He's not a speculator. He views the data and puts it into a system for success. If trying to develop this persona, the ability to have system eyes is the gateway skill. Practice looking at what are things behind the scenes. It doesn't have to be money-related.   How does your favorite TV show come to be? A system of video production, paying the actors, and determining their roles are all systems. Aren't you curious how that all comes together? Give in to your curiosity. The more you can identify and recognize systems, the more this persona is developed if you wish to develop in it.

The preserver

Life has a cycle to it here. Put in work and take your reward. After a while, if you work hard, you're going to have quite a few prizes. These rewards don't just stay afloat. Many of them, you have to keep paying to have access to them. You accept this and keep working for them because they improve your quality of life. This is the motto and mentality of the preserver.

From a young age, she never liked working. Her parents tried, but she just refused to do it. Only after her parents showed her something she really wanted, did she take an interest. They then let her know that this would be hers if she worked for it. The vision of what she wanted fueled her drive to put the work in so she could have it. Ever since then, she realized that the world is full of things she wants. She only needs to put the work in to get them. Sometimes, what she wants costs more in total cash than she has at the time. She wants them, though. They increased her quality of life. Cars, clothes, houses, TVs, furniture, everything; she has no problem with having to finance something if it means she can keep expanding her life at a decent pace. If she were to stop working, then the money would stop. Hence, the payments for some of these things wouldn't get met, and they would disappear. Her instinct is to preserve what she has worked so hard to get.

Some of her friends and family call her somewhat reckless. "You shouldn't finance things! You should try to pay cash." These are the things people say. The truth is they are projecting how they would act in these situations and not realizing how she does act. They buy a TV on a payment plan and get too lazy to pay for it as they are sitting on the couch watching it. They then get mad when it gets taken away and say, "I'm never doing that again." The preserver in that same situation wouldn't be wasting away on that couch. She's already made a financial plan to pay for that TV because she wants to preserve it. This is in her emotional makeup.

Many times, these things she buys aren't just what they are, such as a TV. They represent a stage in her life. Verification that she is moving forward. For it to go away would feel like she is going backward or that her life is contracting. That's the worse feeling in the world to her, and she will put in more work to make sure that doesn't happen. She knows this about herself and will often buy things just as a way to keep her motivated to keep moving forward.

Best income source: OA

The best way of dealing with their emotions: Emotional control

The best way of goal setting: Goal management

The best way of paying bills: Bill management

What makes a preserver: Expenses and self-spending

Expenses or self-spending. It doesn't matter which one comes first or second. If the bulk of the spending in a budget is in expenses and self-spending, this is what makes a preserver. For this persona, having a monthly expense that is attached to you (or family if applicable) is motivating. Every time you use what the expense is paying for, you receive emotional verification that it was worth it. When you get that massage, go to that weekly boot camp, play online on your ps4, etc. These expenses could be one time, but the reoccurring ones create a whole lifestyle together. A lifestyle that you don't mind fighting for. This surprisingly enough makes many people with this persona health nuts. Spending money on themselves as an expense to maintain themselves in some form or fashion. This persona finds it emotionally easy to spend money on themselves and pay their expenses because their expenses play a role in maintaining their lifestyle. Some personal examples of this expense and self-spending are:

I have YouTube premium which makes my YouTube experience ad-free. It cost $11.99 per month. I don't like being interrupted or having to wait to watch a video because of ads. I'm not going back and will make the $$$ to keep YouTube premium. The same goes for my Netflix subscription. I enjoy having access to many movies, shows, and Netflix originals. It's not free to go to my gym. It costs a monthly membership. I'm not a fan of fiction books, but if I was, a subscription to audible would fit here. All of these combine to make a lifestyle full of things that I enjoy and am paying for. Making less money would threaten these in my budget. I don't want that, and this is why I want to keep making the same or more $$$ to preserve this lifestyle type. Below are some examples of activities that are both an expense and self-spending that would be in the preserver's wheelhouse:

1. Paying for a car that you enjoy driving in.

2. Paying for a mortgage to your dream home.

3. You enjoy listening to fictional audiobooks, so you have an audible subscription where you can listen to a certain amount per month for a monthly fee.

4. Using a credit card with a sound point system to pay your expenses, pay back the money before any interest is added, and redeem the points for discounts on things like travel and merchandise.

The preserver's weakness: Investments and savings

Investments and savings are the literally 2 financial areas that deal with the future. One is for financial issues in the future, whether they be unplanned like your transmission going out or planned like retirement. The other being the art of money giving itself back to you in a higher form. The preserver's strength comes from the areas that deal more so in the now. It's emotionally challenging for her to spend money in these areas because of that. That can lead to her being put in a bad situation. If unplanned financial issues come seemingly out of nowhere and there isn't much in savings, you will either have to forget about spending money on yourself, which will be emotionally draining or some bills will get sacrificed. This, in turn, can make things harder than they need to be. Preservers can find themselves in a quagmire. Something always coming up and setting them back, undoing the progress they made, and since there is little to no investments, there isn't any increase in income at a decent pace. To avoid this, try spending money in these two areas BEFORE you spend money in your strength areas. This will ensure that you keep moving forward. As mentioned in a previous chapter, none of the areas should ever drop below 5%. You may also want to consider creating a new income stream to pay for a reoccurring expense BEFORE you get it.

The preserver's special ability

With the ability to work hard and have her emotions engaged at a high level, this creates a unique ability to be very adaptive to financial situations. When we are in a high emotional state, our ability to learn increases, and we retain more information from experience at a more intense level. If this ability were summarized in one word, it would be adaptive. This ability is brought about because out of the 6 personas of the financial world, the preserver is the only one that blends a game plan with high emotion. This is the equivalent of having a full tank of gas and a path set for you to reach your destination or goal. Preservers have the natural ability to morph into and learn what they need to reach their financial goals or preferred lifestyle. This trait is not to be underestimated. Many make a game plan but fail to do anything because they're not emotionally invested. Some have the emotions but not the game plan or willingness to create one. Some have the emotions and a game plan but are too rigid to change the game plan to fit the situation better. The preserver is none of these! They have the emotions, game plan, and the willingness to be adaptive. If trying to develop this persona, think deeply about the preferred lifestyle you want. Focus on why you want that lifestyle so much. You will find that making a game plan is the easy part. Engaging those emotions may be a more significant challenge. If possible, try to experience a portion of the lifestyle you seek in a small dose. If part of that lifestyle is to travel internationally x amount of times per year, go national right now. Do it just to engage and develop this persona. Now would be a great time to revisit your selfish reasons from your list in chapter 3.

The Sniper

Some people simply think but never act. Some people always act without thinking. Would it shock you that some can actually do both? Yes, I know, that's unbelievable, right? The combination of these two attributes gives birth to this persona. Both calculating and volatile, the sniper takes pride in selecting his financial targets with precision based on what he wants. He then makes a plan on how to execute on the details of the mark. Positioning himself at the right distance, at the right place and when the timing is right, he acts going full speed. With successful planning, he hits the target. If he misses, he enters fully on acting mode and moves fast to reposition himself for a chance to hit the target again. Hold on, though these targets are part of a larger target or task. Each time he hits a target; this moves him closer to succeeding in his overall goal. These targets could be several goals that need to be achieved on the way to hitting the ultimate financial goal. They could be tasks that play a role in building a business as a whole.

As calm as the sniper is, he is naturally quite explosive. Equivalent to dynamite that is blowing up. When he acts, it's like an explosion — an intense wave of energy that can move the masses around them. If something is in the way of them achieving a target (goal), they do what they need to get them out of the way so they can move forward on the path to hitting the target. This type of energy almost guarantees success in a goal. So, what's the problem?

This seemingly unlimited explosion of energy can't be sustained. It has an end period. Once it's over, the sniper is burned out and must take time off or at a lower work ethic to recover. What does he do if he burns out in the middle of a mission, before he successfully hit his target? You might as well be hearing cricket sounds. This is why he likes to plan and learn everything about his targets ahead of time. As long as the things that come up are part of the plan, his energy remains intense and explosive. The more obstacles he runs into that were not part of the plan, the higher the chance he will get mentally and physically burned out. That's why he spends as much time, if not more, at planning and researching his targets, then acting. What will happen when I do this? How long will it take to do that? What are the protocols when this happens? He asks questions like this and builds a structure of information, protocols, and procedures he can draw on when needed. The stronger plan and structure he builds, the longer he can maintain his explosive state when it's time to act. He doesn't want to burn out and become lethargic and have to stop to recover. He wants to hit his target and take some recovery time before moving on to his next.

Best income source: UA

The best way of dealing with their emotions: Emotional control

The best way of goal setting: Goal control

The best way of paying bills: Bill control

What makes a sniper: Expenses and savings

When the first and second areas you spend most of your monthly earnings are expenses and savings, you're in the territory of the sniper (no puns intended). If so much of your money is going to expenses, things are tight. The expenses could be your typical bills, or these could be expenses that will make you money in the future. That's irrelevant here though. The point is, they are a large part of your current budget. Since your savings are a big part of your budget also, you must be saving for something. It could just be to build your savings up; it could be saving for something like a new house, starting a business, a new car, or a seminar that's coming up in a few months. Whatever it is, you're putting money away for it. This, by default, gives birth to a target mentality. Paying expenses as they come up and checking your progress on the amount you've saved. These two areas come easily for the sniper because of the mentality they put you in. The mindset described would unsettle some, but it's the home quarters for the sniper. The following are examples of some techniques that he can use to make money off of his strengths, which are paying expense and saving.

1. Paying his expenses with a card that gives him cashback and save that money in a certain account.

2. Looking for savings accounts that have low to no monthly fees while paying high interest, at least being higher than 2% so that the money for long term savings goals cannot lose value to inflation and your monthly expenses remain low.

3. Contributing to a traditional or SEP IRA retirement account, you use as long term savings and writing off the contributions off your taxes, reducing them for that year.

4. Paying a knowledgeable tax professional to file your taxes and save you more money than you could if filing yourself due to their knowledge of the laws.

The sniper's weaknesses: Investments and self-spending

If the sniper's strengths are expenses and savings, his weaknesses would be investing and self-spending. He has tunnel vision. Expense and savings are milestones all part of that vision to get him to his ultimate goal. These two areas can escape his attention. He sees his ultimate goal which will take a while (at least over a month) to complete, hence the reason his savings plan exists. Investments give a more immediate return but maybe smaller. He either deems the return not worth distracting him off his current course, or he doesn't want to invest the time in what's needed to make the investment work. Spending money on investments is the art of having your money come back to you with a little extra to it. Without it, your financial life tends to stagnate. The sniper does often end up getting ahead due to his hard work and savings goal, but it takes longer due to his ignoring of investments.

Since he is so good at cutting off his emotions, he'll pretty much ignore himself too when it comes to self-spending. In his mind, he rather just put the extra money to his savings so he can reach his goal quicker. I can't stress this enough. You don't want any of the financial areas to drop below 5%. If the sniper does not spend some money on himself, he'll run the risk of burning out sooner and unexpectedly. Self-spending is good for your emotional health. Just because you can cut your emotions off for a duration of time doesn't mean you're not feeling them. You're just so externalized that you're not focused on them. When you spend money on things that you like, it is a small emotional recovery in itself. This needs to be remembered, and while it may seem that you don't have the time for investments, respect the role it plays in moving your financial life forward and allocate money to it.

If you find yourself neglecting these areas, then spend your budgeted money on your investment area first before you spend on anything else. Spread out the self-spending throughout the month so they can serve as small recover sessions. Almost a year after getting promoted to PA at amazon, I was ready to get back to the business world. Most of my money was going to savings and expenses. The savings were for the business. I felt fine at work but started feeling down at home. Every once in a while, I would spend some of my hard-earned money that was gonna go to savings on myself. I felt a lot better afterward. Without spending money on yourself, you feel like a slave regardless of the situation. I also had the chance to take various courses on things I had interest in like real estate and stocks. These would be considered investments. I ignored them because I just wanted to focus on my goal. Ironically later in my life, I did take courses on these subjects, but I would have reached my financial goals faster if I obtained that knowledge in those courses sooner. The bottom line is if you're in this persona, don't neglect these areas. Ignoring them has subtle but strong consequences.

The sniper's special ability

The sniper, at his core, is both active and devising. Those combined give him the ability to make financial structures and protocols to achieve his goals. He creates them in such a way to where they can be upgraded fast and easy when he receives new information and learns something new. This is different from the builder. Where the builder builds a very rigid system, which is an attempt to be perfect, the sniper's structure is designed not to be perfect. They are designed with him knowing it will most likely need to be updated at some point. They are intended to be the backbone of his activity.

A good example of this is a plumber that is familiar with how things are set up in a house. Some things are fundamental to a smooth plumbing system. At the same time, each one is different, so he has procedures in place to deal with those differences on the spot. This is what separates the builder and the sniper. I know you're wondering why I'm comparing the two personas so much. It needs to be done because they are somewhat alike. Both of them build and utilizes financial structures. The main difference between the two is that the builder's structure is a system that ultimately manages money while the sniper's structure is made to support his activity when he is putting work in directly. That's why the best income for the builder is OP, and the best for the sniper is UA. Bringing it back to his unique ability, in a nutshell; it is the ability to set up protocols that support his active activity, so he encounters minimal obstacles he can't deal with. In doing these things, this gives the literal laser lighting that a sniper rifle gives off when pointed at the target, knowing when and why they are aiming for this specific target at this time. Some of the other personas may find it challenging to focus on one thing and THEN move on to the next. This is the sniper's greatest strength.

The Fame Seeker

When you are thinking or daydreaming, do you see yourself being the center of attention? If you do, you may be a sleeping fame seeker! In most cases, we are the center of attention in our thought. This persona just has it much stronger than the others. Coming from a mindset of abundance, she seeks to enjoy and experience all that life has to offer. In doing so, she also wants to do her part in the world.

From a young age, she always liked to be the center of attention. In her head, she would see someone do something; then she would play that same scenario in her head except with her being at the center of it instead of the other person. This is the person that would be daydreaming in class. When asked what they are thinking about by their friends, the conversation would end up being about them and their dreams. Before long, she realized that she couldn't be the center of attention in everything because she doesn't know or can't do everything. This craving for attention didn't go away, though. She had to find some kind of outlet for it to come out that doesn't come off as snobby and conceited. Through this self-reflection, she discovered that she had a talent for something. She would do it, and people enjoyed her doing it. She was also very good at it. Doing the things she had the talent for got her all the attention she craves, but then it's going back to the same boring life. A frown goes across her face. Then she realized, what if there was a way that she could monetize her talent. She could be getting paid to do what she loves!

On top of this, it would also be filling the attention void that she has. That's what she does, and she lives a life of abundance. Since she can make more money by simply doing what she loves and has a talent for, she feels all her financial problems can be solved simply by monetizing more of her ability. It could be her talent using technology, performing, public speaking, designing, etc. Her natural wanting for attention is more than just merely the attention itself. Every time she does something she is talented at, she received money and complements for a job well done.

In some cases, those complements and recognition of her talents and values are worth far more than the money. When she gets validation from others, she feels an emotion high. That emotional high can be used to work even more to make more money; hence, the cycle repeats! The fame seeker sees the world not from one paycheck to another but from one experience to another.

Best income source: UA

The best way of dealing with their emotions: Emotional autopilot

The best way of goal setting: Freeflow goals

The best way of paying bills: Bill autopay

What makes a fame seeker: Self-spending and investments

You've probably guessed that these would be the two areas that would make a fame seeker. What else screams of that abundant mindset we mentioned earlier? She loves to spend that money that she made using her talent on herself. It keeps her on that emotional high, which in turn, keeps making her money. She is the most emotional out of the 6 personas, followed by the preserver. She also likes to spend money on things that will bring more money to her. These can be tangible things, but investing in items that affect the way she feels is an even bigger investment for her. She has the mentality that the universe will bring her what she focuses on, and since she focuses on money, she will buy things that symbolize it. This could be a robe that has money on it, dollar bill pillows, or $$$ screensaver on her phone. These are little subtle rituals that bring her more wealth and can be pulled from both the self-spending and investments in the budget. What's the second or arguably 1st biggest thing that she can spend on herself that affects how she feels for the better? Health! The fame seeker can turn out to be quite the health junkie. Spending money on juicers, vitamixs, detoxes, anything that improves her health and likewise, how she feels. The following are some examples of activities that are both self-spending and investment that would be in the fame seeker's wheelhouse.

1. Going to have a massage done.

2. Buying things that increase the quality of her health in terms of how she feels.

3. Buying clothes or items that remind her of $$$ like money robes or caps that put and keep her in an abundance mindset.

4. Buying casual things that have to do with how you make money. For example, if you're a popular YouTuber, you might buy a pillow that looks like a subscribe button.

5. Searching for cashback opportunities when you go on vacation.

The fame seeker's weaknesses: Expenses and Savings

There is a reoccurring theme with investments and self-spending being strengths. One of them keeps you in the future, and the other keeps you in the feeling of the now. The spending of money always brings money to you in the future. Savings and expenses are more or less about maintaining one's financial self. The fame seeker can be emotionally disinterested in these two areas. If she is indifferent, she won't give them much attention. This can lead to paying more; then you should on some expenses. Where a little planning or shopping around for the right deal could save hundreds of dollars on expenses literally, they just don't want to spend the time doing it.

Ironically, any saved money that comes from doing this could be used to spend on themselves and investments. They know this but are often not interested. Wanna know why? When you spend money on yourself, how do you feel? When you spend money on something you know will give you some kind of return, how do you feel? A lot of people feel great! There is an emotional boost from spending in these areas. Spending on expenses and savings are about maintaining one's financial self. That psychological boost is not the case for expenses that impact the now and savings that impact the future. How do you feel when spending money on these? People tend to feel more secure. The fame seeker isn't the persona known for insecurity though. That's why they have little to no interest in these areas. It's okay if you're not interested in an area or two. You shouldn't neglect them though. Sure, you can, but there will be consequences. A good thing for the fame seeker to do is to have their expense spending and savings as autonomous as possible. That means that it can just be taken care of and they can check on it periodically. In some cases, they may even not like putting money in these areas. They may consider it bringing down their emotional state. This will help to deal with that. Realize that you don't have to love them, but you should not neglect them either.

The fame seeker's special ability

With her high receptivity to her emotions, she has the special ability of creativity. Yes, everyone has the creativity to a certain degree, but hers is on steroids. It's because she can use her talent to make money, so this requires her always to be engaging her emotions. This is done by being receptive to the ideas around her and intergrading them into her routines and tasks.

Creativity is the use of the imagination to accomplish something when it comes to the financials. This mindset spills over into finances in general and doesn't just stay in her career. Once she starts flowing, she may find herself coming up with quicker ways to do mundane tasks and even coming up with financial formulas that she can use to achieve her vast dreams. Many people would be more creative, but strong creativity requires momentum. Since most people don't have a steady demand for it, they may be creative just to accomplish one thing. Then there is not a need for it, so the momentum dies. With the fame seeker, her income is tied to her creativity and personality. This supplies an endless demand for it and likewise, a continuous momentum streak! She can challenge herself to come up with fast and fun ways to do things.

This book is yet another example of this. Writing a book may seem boring to some. It's not for me, but it wasn't necessarily stimulating either. I started out writing 2 pages a day and would not do anything else until they were written. That was yielding good results, but then I got an idea to make a playlist that I only listen to when writing for the book. The playlist is about 2 hours and 30 minutes long. All of a sudden, I found myself writing faster because music helps my thoughts flow. I also started writing 5 to 6 pages a day. Sometimes, I would write an entire chapter. I would just keep going until the playlist was done. When I wasn't in the mood to write, I would start playing that playlist, and within a few minutes, I was typing away. This is an example of how I took a mundane task and made it exciting and got better results. That required creativity, and that is the specialty of the fame seeker.

The King of the hill

Have you ever met the type of person that has no problem doing what others are financially afraid of? You may be one of them. The kind of person that recognizes and respects the risks for something, but the rewards motivate them far past the fear of those risks. Someone who seems to be a natural leader and makes money because of it? The person who seems to be charismatic without even trying? This is the domain of the king of the hill. If the 6 personas had elemental signs like the zodiac, the sniper and the king of the hill would definitely be fire signs. The quality of fire would be different though. Where the sniper is more of an explosive type, powerful like dynamite in short bursts than needing to recover, the king of the hill is of a different breed. The fire here is a very very strong, almost overwhelming steady fire that burns consistently like the sun. It's not as intense as the explosive fire of the sniper, but that's why it is steady. He has a goal or a mission financially and is willing to work very hard to reach it.

He is the type that doesn't start off with small goals and works up to the bigger ones. He wants a big goal from the start. If he is focused and see to it that he keeps his vitality strong, then he can be very strong-willed and will persevere until the goal is reached. To achieve these big goals, he will put himself in uncomfortable positions so that he can get there faster. He has a proper assessment of his self-development. He wouldn't put himself on the train yard to work without having any previous training, but he would be willing to advance at a faster pace than most because he is an overachiever.

He's the type that doesn't shy away from leadership positions; he actively looks for them. Since he has such big goals, he realizes that he can't reach them alone at a reasonable pace. Therefore, he will work with people and manage them in ways to achieve the mission or goal. While he is self-confident, he realizes and respects the role other people play in his financial life. Since he cares about the people that are connected to him financially and he knows how to delegate, manage and work with others, people see him or put him in the leadership positions he craves so that the goal(s) can be achieved. Because of this, he is often not successful unless his team is successful, so he works to make sure everyone is pushing forward towards the goal. Making sure they are taken care of emotionally and achieving their own individual goals because it benefits the whole. This isn't the dull Hank Hill from the TV show a few years back. This is the kind of the financial hill!

Best income source: OA

Best way of dealing with their emotions: Emotional management

Best way of goal setting: Goal management

Best way of paying bills: Bill management

The 2 types of kings

There are two stages of this persona. One leads into the other in many cases, except for when someone has these personality traits and are put in leadership positions from a young age. The first stage is not being the king in terms of leadership and social situations but rather staying on top of your stuff. What I mean by on top of your stuff is you know where you are financially at all times. You know how much free money you have right now. You know how much debt you are in and how much on each account. You know how far away you are from paying that debt off. You have your financial goals set and are actively working to acquire the money or skills to reach them. You are the king of your own hill or on top of your life.

This persona more than any of the others is more in tune with his finances and looks at them the most regularly. It is vital to his personality. Each time he does, he gets verification of where he is and if changes need to be made. Where the others may do this weekly or monthly, this persona has no problem doing it daily. Some kings stay in this first stage, and there is nothing wrong with that. They are sole kings. They are just the king of their own hill as opposed to being responsible for others.

The second stage is when he is directly responsible for others financially to a certain extent but also emotionally. This includes managing, motivating, and guiding others who are on his team. If you are in stage 1 and you are successful with managing your own finances and goals, which reflects in you reaching them, society will find a way to put you into a leadership role, which will boost you into stage 2. The only way it won't happen is if you resist against it by showing a disinteresting in being responsible for others. As mentioned before, there is nothing wrong with staying in stage 1 but realize that stage 2 offers larger rewards then stage 1 because the scope of it is bigger. For example, if you're producing a movie, you could try and do everything by yourself and make a semi-decent project with a modest return, or you can put together the right team and produce something high quality which is much better and gives a HUGE gain for everyone involved, including you. Both scenarios require skills in your wheelhouse. One just offers a much bigger return for you but also more interpersonal and management skills. Which one you want is up to you.

What makes a king of the hill: Investments and expenses

The king of the hill knows and respects the fact that in order to make money in the future, it requires a combination of spending money on things that make you money in the now, as well as the future. It isn't a universal principle of money, but it works well for this persona. Since he is good at staying on top of his finances, he manages his expenses well. In addition to this, he always has plans to divert the resources needed to a place that will yield a specific result he needs, i.e., investments. After operating like this for a bit, he realizes (whether it be consciously or subconsciously) that he can get greater results by combining the two. Why not spend money on something that is an expense and giving him a return? Pay a small value in exchange for a bigger benefit in the future.

This comes in the form of finding ways to get money from his spending on expenses. A personal example I can give is a card I use to get my gas, which is a reoccurring expense. The money is going into the expense column every month. This card offers cashback for using it. I get cash every month back via cashback, and I can use that money to fund something else, let's say an investment! The king of the hill also will actively seek out things that will help him achieve his goal but costs money. Even if it is a reoccurring expense, he knows it will help him get what he wants or make more money. This has the potential to make him very good at managing debt since he develops the ability to use that money to make more money via acting on the right opportunity.

It's the same for other monthly expenses too. The following are some examples:

1. If a platform costs a monthly fee to have access to it.

2. If there is a membership to a community that helps him and has a monthly fee.

3. If he needs a monthly coaching session to keep him on track with his plan which costs $.

4. If he needs a consultation to answer some questions in an area he is weak in. He will make these calls without having a long mental conversation with himself.

A personal example for me is morningstar.com premium; it has tools and information that is extremely useful to a long term investor, but with a monthly fee. This is something I don't mind paying because it helps me make more money and spend less time on my investments.

Literally on the flip side, he values expenses, and if an expense doesn't meet a particular value, he doesn't mind putting in some work himself to reduce or eliminate the expense. When my brakes needed to be replaced, I knew the dealership would charge around $500 to change the front and rear pads. I found this to be a joke. I don't care much for car mechanics, but I wasn't about to pay that. I talked to one of my friends who is car savvy, and he told me about an old mechanic he found on craigslist that changes $60 for putting on brake pads. He actually lived in my city too. You just needed to bring the brakes, so I bought the brakes at auto zone for $58 and set an appointment with him. I spent a total of $118 for his labor and the brakes. That took more time, but I didn't mind because that $500 expense was not worth that value, so I was willing to make it up in some extra time for a better deal. This screams of the king of the hill persona!

The spending on investments and expenses is one of the subtle things that keep the king of the hill on top of his game and moving forward. Some examples of activities that are both an expense and an investment that would be in the king's wheelhouse are as follows:

1. Paying more money on a monthly expense like a car note than the minimum and apply the excessive income to the principal, effetely shortening the time you will be in debt for it. Down the road, this will result in an increase in income due to the cashflow that was being used to pay for it is now available for other things. This, in turn, is an investment that will reduce or eliminate a reoccurring expense.

2. Attending a paid class on a subject you're weak in financially. It is an expense that is giving you a return on your money later, making it an investment also.

3. Paying a conferencing software like go to meetings or zoom conference, a monthly fee for something that allows you to host conferencing calls with your team. This helps you train your team and is both an investment and an expense.

4. Paying a licensing fee for a music subscription site like epidemic sounds, so that you can use their music in your productions.

The king of the hill's weaknesses: Savings and self spending

With the king of the hill being so externalized, he can often glaze over spending money on himself in the form of self-spending. He can be so focused on everything that is happening on the outside of himself; he may neglect what he is feeling internally when faced with a decision. Do I spend this money on an investment or on myself? Most of the time, the first one will win. There's nothing wrong with prioritizing investments and expenses; don't keep neglecting yourself though

On the same token, since he is usually successful with managing a balance of expenses and investments, they tend to bring him returns. It can be a quagmire of him spending money on expenses and investments and getting money from that spending later and repeating the cycle. Remember that things happen and savings are needed. It can often be undervalued since money can be flowing in from your activities. That is a mistake. Don't neglect your savings. That's the cushion you need if the rug is pulled right from under you suddenly in the form of some unplanned financial setback.

The king of the hill's special ability

It's been brought up in the whole section, but his unique ability is his leadership capabilities. People trust him to manage and lead things to the result everyone wants. Leadership is bringing out the best in people, and it's something that he does by default. He wants everyone around him to reach their maximum potential and is willing to help them in that process. What is truly special though is he is very good at finding ways to monetize this.

A good example of this is I've seen people on YouTube give classes on investing in stocks. They offer courses, and once in the course, students get one-on-one attention and Q & As. Their portfolios are public, and they work with their students to achieve their goals. I also know some network marketers who are truly sincere in helping their downline move passed their emotional challenges to make the kind of money they want. These are scenarios where someone is leveraging their leadership skills and getting paid for it. Finding out a way to do this is a feat within itself. There is a balance between having a charismatic personality and being that a person people can relate to by teaching the information, methods, and procedures that the person needs. The king of the hill has this locked down once he has developed it and, the good news is the need for this will never go away. There will always be people who need to be taught, coached, and encouraged by this type of persona. You need only to find ways to monetize it.

The Conservative

We all have our preferences when it comes to what kind of person we like to be romantically involved with. Sure, we have small things that we like or don't like in general, but there are always things that at the core you simply can't put up with or must have in a mate. I can't be with someone who lies. My mate has to do xyz for me. If you want more examples, just go hang out with your friends and bring up relationships. What would be your response if I told you that the same is true for how we earn and spend our money too? Isn't that a big surprise?

We all have those financial values that we must have at our core, and things we don't want to settle for. We sometimes have to put those core values aside and do what we need to do to make ends meet. Not the conservative. This part of her is much stronger than everyone else. She has a vision or thought of how a financial scenario should be in her life, and she won't compromise on having that vision even if it means going through hard financial times. These core values are so important to her that she will many times choose to conserve them at the cost of other things financially.

I have friends with this personality type who will never work a job again. At their core, what they value more than anything financially is the freedom to pursue what they want and however they want. I bring this up not to crap on traditional employment but rather to illustrate the point of how the conservative functions. If we dig deeper, though, her value(s) that she is conserving is just a conduit for something else. At the core, it is an emotional state. In this, we find that she has a strong desire to either stay in a current emotional state or avoid a particular one. For example, my friends, who are so opposed to jobs, have different situations. One of them wants to maintain an emotional state. That state being peace. She doesn't like being told what to do, nor does she like being supervised. She is very good at what she does and feels she doesn't need

214

supervision. Truth be told, she doesn't. She knows that being in these situations, she will say things that would be the most inappropriate. In doing so, she would feel emotions that take her out of her preferred emotional state, hence her desire to conserve the peaceful state by not getting in that situation.

I have another friend who seeks to avoid an emotional state. He hopped from job to job before he found his passion in starting his own business. He would always be working harder than most, only to see slackers get ahead. This, in turn, would make him very angry. If he works hard, he expects to be paid more eventually. He also understands that if he doesn't work hard, he doesn't deserve to be paid much. He is conserving the emotional state of passion by avoiding that scenario. The conservative can wait for years, struggling to make ends meet, feeling and enduring every other negative emotion, maybe even the same feeling that she is actively avoiding. She is willing to do that as long as it's not the same environment as what she dreads.

She looks and waits for the right opportunity, scenario, or situation where she can work and make money doing what she wants in her preferred mental state. It is the way she functions. Because of this, she leads with her emotions first and everything else last. She will think of how she wants to feel and make a scenario from there to how she can make money. Once she does this, this vision is burned in her mind and emotions. She won't settle for anything else. Most would consider this crazy, but this is indeed the 1st step towards getting what you want. Only after you've done this, you will not only start to see the potential opportunities that are good for you but they also start coming to you. The conservative on some level knows this, and she tends to be a magnet, pulling things gradually that help her make that perfect scenario until it's formed.

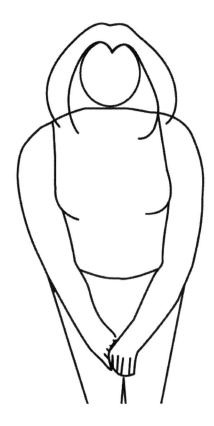

The best income source: UP

The best way of dealing with their emotions: Emotional Autopliot

The best way of goal setting: Goal control

The best way of paying bills: Bill control

What makes a conservative: Self spending and savings

Are you surprised by this? The conservative wants to conserve herself emotionally in the short term and long term. The short term is spending money on herself and the long term being saving money. Her self-spending goes beyond the simple splurging or the "I have to have that" syndrome. She recognizes and respects the impact that spending money on herself has on her emotional state. The truth is she can go without spending money on herself. The longer she goes without doing it though, the more stressed and voided she feels. If you spend money on everything except for the self area, you will feel a void in yourself. Self-spending is a way that serves as revalidation that we are heading in the right direction; both for ourselves and our work. The conservative knows this and will spend money on herself if she deems it emotionally necessary.

She also knows that there will be times of hardship that she may have to endure on the way to her ideal financial circumstances happening. That's why she is a good saver. That and if an opportunity becomes available that can deliver her the financial scenario she seeks and it costs money, she wants to be able to take advantage of it. With these two areas being her strength, it would strengthen both of them to find ways that you can spend and save at the same time. For example, there is an app called acorns that has deals with many businesses where if you buy from them and you use acorn, they will invest a % of your purchase or a flat rate in your account. There are well over 100 businesses on there and growing. Imagine if you checked there before making a purchase and it's there, then you buy what you want through the app. You'll take that extra money you are getting back in your acorns account and save it. Tactics like this are the playground of the conservative. Some examples of activities that are both savings and self-spending that would be in the conservative's wheelhouse are below:

1. Using an app like acorns to buy things for yourself and get money invested in a mutual fund portfolio automatically, which you can later withdraw from. Note that this would only be if you spend enough to make the $1 monthly management fee they charge ultimately insignificant.

2. Linking the app called earny to a debit/credit card and having it track your purchases and find the lowest price. Then it refunds you the

difference between the amount you paid and the lower price. You then save that money.

3. Paying for your self-spending with a credit card that has a great point system. Make the payments before any interest is acquired. Then redeem those points for cashback and save that money.

4. Using the tactic of credit card churning. Find a credit card with the right point sign on bonus that gets you free travel and hotel costs. Apply and get the credit card. Save up the amount of money that needs to be spent so you can get the bonus. Put a large payment on a reoccurring expense like the mortgage or car payment on the credit card. Use the saved money to pay off the card on time, so you don't pay any interest. Then enjoy your free vacation.

The conservative's weaknesses: Investments and expenses

The conservative sees these two areas as one that takes money without a significant enough return and the other as a necessary evil. She can mentally go back and forth on if she wants to spend money on investments. Whether her savings are for emergencies or if she is saving for something big in the future, she sees that as being a much bigger return in the future, more so than an investment can give her now. Remember that part of that return includes her emotional state now and then. Saving money helps her emotional state now. Meanwhile, investing doesn't. That's why she habitually puts the money in savings and not investing. News flash! Investments are what produce a middle ground between being financially good and financially struggling. They give back in the more near future. This, in turn, helps you in one or more ways financially. That is partly why the conservative can go through unneeded financial struggles that is not taking place.

As far as expenses go, she sees them as something that just has to be done. When having to choose between expenses and savings or self-spending, the last two are normally picked. This is the person that will stare at the screen of a bill for minutes before paying it. This isn't saying that's a bad thing, but rather the expenses need to be valued for what they are paying for. A different outlook will help with this and help keep that emotional state, which is so vital to this persona staying in good standing.

The conservative's special ability

Have you heard of penny-pinching before? Take that concept and make it less cheap or more creative. The conservative can dig deep to find ways to keep herself afloat and save money for herself to seize the perfect money scenario when it presents itself. That includes cutting the budget down, using coupons, finding deals, and looking for something financially that fills her values. As mentioned before, many don't have the stomach to weather the storm before they reach paradise. Don't underestimate this trait. There have been many people who have adopted this conservative mentality to achieve their dreams, and these are millionaires. It's the ability to be uncompromising in what you accept for yourself financially, and it is engraved in her very being. With that being the case, it seems to pull the things she needs indirectly. The movie "The Secret" goes heavy into this when they talk about the wave you send out to the universe. The conservative is in tune with herself to such a degree that she knows what values she is conserving at all times. She can also detect when they are or have changed. Most people go through life, and their value simply changes. Since your values are what ultimately drive you, then they should be known by you at all times. How else will you know where to look for what you want when they do change?

The conservative is so synced with her emotional state when something takes her out of what she wants to be; she refers to her values. If there is a contradiction, she reevaluates why she feels that way. This results in values getting updated or replaced. The cycle then repeats again! This is a persona that rarely suffers from having a void inside. Her values are simply too up to date for that.

We have now covered the 6 personalities that make up the financial world. Now, it is time to use this information in a constructive way.

CHAPTER 10.

STRATEGIC MANAGEMENT:

HOW TO BUDGET ACCORDING TO YOUR PERSONALITY

We all have strengths and weaknesses when it comes to finances. It is the awareness of these that allow you to put the right focus on the right things at that time so that you ensure you're always moving forward. As mentioned before, each one of the 6 personas has a goal style, emotion style, and bill pay style. Many times over, people get themselves in trouble with their budget by using the wrong technique based on their personality. Have you ever linked a bill to your bank account only to realize you forget you did? Then your account is charged next month, and you get pissed because it was unexpected. That may work good for one person but not that great for another. Part of being financially savvy is knowing what style of management works best for you when it comes to money. I said in the last chapter that we would cover the goal, bill and emotional styles here. Since we have finally arrived here, let's go into it.

Strategic Management

Although many people try to make the dynamics of budget management seem like such a complex task, it's not that complicated. We already know about the areas of a budget. What about the ways we manage our budget, goals, and bills. Would it shock you to find out this varies from person to person? Most likely not. We all have things we prioritize over other things. This is reflected in what areas of our budget we spend the most on which is a reflection of our personality as we covered the last chapter. We will now look at the 3 budgeting techniques of a budget.

A budgeting technique is simply a way you go about executing your budget. Whether we realize it or not, we are juggling these 3 things in a budget: How you pay bills, how you spend for things and how you manage doing what you like vs. making more money. If we condense these into a few words, we have bills, goals, and rewards. Bills are self-explanatory. What isn't is how do you pay them? Do you have your bank account linked and they are paid automatically? Do you pay them with a debit card when they are due? Do you pay with a check? These vary often depending on the person.

Goals are the 5/6 areas of the budget. How precise or general are they? Does the person have money budgeted for the self area and spend money as they want or do they have multiple things in the budget that is just categorized as self? Do they have a hair appointment, video game, massage and speed dating, all separate in their budget but fall under the self area? Rewards are us indulging in what we want emotionally.

After a hard day's work, it's time to hope on the ps4! We all know that we could be using this time to make more money. We want to make more money, but we also want to indulge in our emotions? Which to pick? If I indulge, I'll never get ahead, but if I keep working, I won't have any fun? The break-even point for us is to do enough work that we deem acceptable and then indulge in our emotions. In doing it this way, the indulgence serves as a reward or recover. How we manage this process varies from person to person.

I know, you're thinking "Enough with the suspense already! Get into the good stuff!" The good stuff as you are thinking is that we all come up with ways to deal with all of these. Bills, goals, and rewards are all governed by one of these three techniques. These techniques are born based off of what we want at the core when it comes to the management of our bills, goals and rewards. We want these things either to be handled autonomously, managed, or to be in direct control of them. One of these three ways of handling them will be best for our personality and how we earn income. Before we go there though, you have to know what your "rewards" are.

Assignment 1

We all have things that we enjoy doing. These things take up time, though. This same time can be devoted to our goals and finding other ways to make money. We can't just abandon our goals and play around all the time. On the same token, does that mean we should just not do things we like to do? Where's the balance between the two? Make a list of things that you enjoy doing regularly. Note that the list shouldn't be that long. If two things are similar, rope them into one big category and put that one category on the list. For example, I enjoy watching Netflix and Amazon video. I would not put both of them on the list. Instead, I would just put "Streaming services" since that's what they both are. Your list should not be more than 8 things. The things on the list should be reoccurring things you do.

At the very least, monthly, and at the very most daily. This means that if you were to randomly decide that you want to go to six flags to have some fun, that wouldn't be on the list because you don't do that on the regular. It would only make the list if you went on a weekly or monthly basis. While athletic activities may fit the criteria, if they are vital to your overall exercise plan or routine for staying healthy and in shape, reframe from adding them on the list unless they are purely fun. I enjoy jogging to the gym, working out, and jogging home. This is part of my regular exercise routine. Even though I enjoy it, the fact that it's critical to maintaining my quality of health keeps it from making the list. You'll understand why this is in a few paragraphs. At the same time, if I want to go down to the park and play some basketball, this activity would make the list because I don't consider it as part of my workout routine. I would be there solely for the fun of it. My exercise needs are being met in another way. This will be what is known as your rewards list for demonstration purposes. Here is my list.

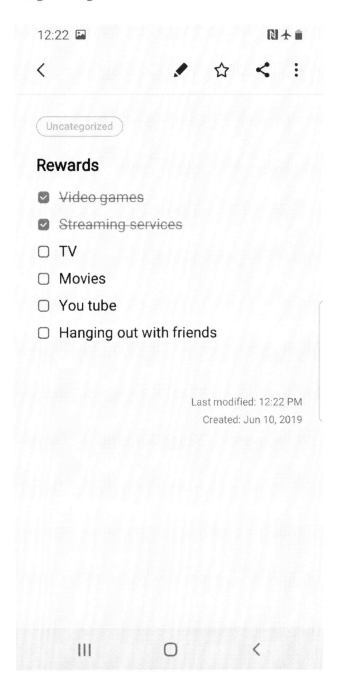

Put this list in your phone where notes are kept. There are plenty of note apps out there like Evernote or memo that you can use to put this list in. Why is this list essential, you may ask? This list puts into context all the things that you use to distract yourself as well as what you use as mental recover. Based on your personality, there is a way that you use the items or activities on this list to mentally recover or sustain yourself while at the same time, minimizing or eliminating using them as distractions. One of the three ways of dealing with your emotions will accomplish this for you. These next sections of this chapter should be viewed as something to be implemented, which will help you with that particular area. At the end of each technique, which persona the technique works best for will be mentioned.

Dealing with our emotions

Technique one: Emotional control

We all know that making more money requires effort. What happens if we keep putting in that effort with no rest. Eventually, you're just going to keel over. At the very least, you will be an irritable and short-tempered person. We know this, which is why we give ourselves moments to indulge in the things we like to recover. Watch TV, Netflix, read books, play video games, go hiking, etc. These are little rituals that we do to rejuvenate ourselves physically and mentally. This exact process is what happens here. This person puts in the work to be in control of their bills and has their goals broken down into individual ones that need to be accomplished one by one. This requires them to be in a work mode for a long time, and at their core, that is their emotional strength!

They can go long periods just working as long as they can recover afterward before getting back to it. For example, someone using this control technique can go to their job and work 8 hours, get home and work another 2 hours, then have the rest of the day to themselves, doing the things they love to recover. Since the things they do for fun are vital to their recovery, they should do any of them they want (with reasons of course). It's all about work and recharging here. This is for those that can work for an exceptionally long time on making money.

At the core, they don't need the emotional recharge of short-term rewards to work for money, and as such, their emotions don't influence them to stop working so they can do fun things. Because of this, they feel that once the amount of time they've assigned for the work is done, then they are free to indulge those emotions in all the ways they would like. They have access to all the things on their reward list after the work is done. It's for the emotionally disciplined. They have the skillset to cut their emotions off for periods of time. If you find yourself getting distracted by your emotions to do non-money making things (get on the Xbox, watch Netflix originals, go swimming, etc.) and you easily give in to them, this way is not going to work out the best for you.

What do you do if you do not reach your financial goal that month? Grab a stopwatch or download a stopwatch app. For every month that you don't hit your financial goals, take 30 minutes of your free time each day, and devote it to researching ways of making money. It should be done every time you do not hit your monthly goal. That means that if you keep not obtaining your goal, you'll have to give more and more of your free time each month. The next time you hit your monthly goal, go back to normal where all the free time you designated is free to do what you want. Yes, this will take discipline, but it is playing towards your strengths. It also ensures that you keep moving financially forward towards your goals. Emotional control works best with the sniper and preserver personas.

Technique two: Emotional autopilot

The emotional autopilot can be seen as the exact opposite of the emotional control method. While the source of strength there comes from cutting your emotions off, the strength here is from fully indulging them. Here, we embrace the fact that we want to play our video games, watch our movies, use our streaming services (Amazon video, Netflix, Hulu, etc.), play our sports. We like to do the things our emotions enjoy and don't want to have access to them. We work for money so we can pay our house note. We enjoy our house, don't we? Same goes for a car we like. It is this strength and attachment to things we enjoy that we are going to use to our advantage. At the beginning of each month, you have access to all of your reward list. As the month goes on, you need to hit certain income milestones. If you don't, one of the things on your list has to get crossed out.

How do you determine the income milestones? Simple. Take your monthly income goal for that month and divide it by the number of things on your list. For me, I have 6 things on my list, so my monthly income would be divided by 6. 4,000$ ÷ 6 = $666.66. Add this number on top of itself 6 times, writing down each number as you do it. Next, divide the number of days in that month by the same number. I always use 30 days.

Yes, there are months with 31 days and February being the odd one out has 28 days with the occasional 29 days but I rather keep it simple. Feel free to use the exact days you want. $30 \div 6 = 5$. Repeat the same process with the days as you did with your income. Line up the days with the income in a chart-like form.

- 5 days: $666.66

- 10 days: $1333.32

- 15 days: $1999.98

- 20 days: $2666.64

- 25 days: $3333.3

- 30 days: $4000

If I were using the emotional autopilot strategy, if I were not at $666.66 within 5 days of the month starting, I would have to cut off something on my reward list. I would lose access to that reward for the rest of the month. If I do hit the income goal, my reward list remains untouched. It is directly using our emotion's desire to have access to the things we like in our favor, effectively aligning that desire with our financial goals. Remember, if you did the assignment in chapter 8, your monthly income should be rising, and this is a motivation to keep it growing. This will require discipline to some degree. If you don't hit your milestones, you'll have to have developed the discipline to not indulge in that reward for the rest of the month. If this is a struggle at first, review your goal list in regards to your preferred lifestyle. Acknowledge that this is needed to ensure you keep moving towards it. Do this every time you feel this being a struggle, and it will take the sting out of it. If this is still a struggle after doing this, I would recommend that you revisit chapter 3 "The will to raise income" as this is a sign that the force behind your desire for a better quality of life is not strong enough.

What do you do if you don't hit your monthly financial goal? Take one of the things on your rewards list and take it off. That activity is off-limits until you reach your monthly goal again. For every month you don't reach your goal, you lose another reward on your list. If you were not to hit the goal for 8 months straight, you might very well be without any actives! Something tells me you're not going to let that happen, right? You still run the drill to see your income milestones and reward unlocks. You'll be doing it with the new number though. For example, if I didn't hit my goal last month, a reward would be removed, and the new number I would use would be 5. This means the interval between milestones will be more. Use this time that would have been spending on your activities to make more money instead. If you hit your monthly goal at any time, your reward list should get reset back to how it was when you started.

"What about if I'm doing things that will make me money later, but it isn't now"? Yes, this is a valid question. Some examples of this would be going to school, the writing of this book, making a YouTube account and videos, looking for real estate deals, etc. These activities take time but most likely won't make you money that month. Activities like this are still moving you towards your financial goals. To intergrade them into this system, get a stopwatch or download the stopwatch app. Anytime you are doing these activities, start the time. When you stop doing the activity, stop the watch. When you reach 10 hours if you have lost a reward due to not hitting a milestone, regain that reward. If you hit 20 hours, you can recover another reward. It maxes out at 20 hours though. Yes, I hate to say it, but all of this will once again take discipline. Stay focused on the vision of your preferred lifestyle, and it will help you stick to this system. Emotional autopilot works best with the fame seeker and conservative personas.

Technique three: Emotional management

There are those of us that are go-getters. We are used to the following pattern. We do work in some form. Then we reap the rewards it brings. I know you're probably thinking, isn't that everyone? No. If you recall in the emotional autopilot, many people do things to maintain what they have, not necessarily going to get new things. At some point, they would have had to get them via working for it but the emotional trigger there is more so on maintaining. A go-getter is more or less always chasing things they don't currently have. In doing so, they prioritize working for what they want over things that they have fun with. They don't cut them off like the emotional control type though. They realize and respect the role they play in their emotional state. Indulging in things they like without doing a certain amount of work actually brings this person a degree of voidness, so they need to be making constant progress towards their goals. It's part of their emotional makeup. Like anyone though, if they don't indulge in the things they like, they will burn out. Due to this, they tend to put in work towards their goals, and once a certain amount of work has been done, they give themselves leeway to do some of the things they enjoy. It's a powerful way of management, and at its core, that's exactly what it is. It is managing their emotions so that they don't get in the way but rather using them to serve as motivation for things. How do we apply this here? We reverse the roles from the emotional autopilot. Instead of having all the rewards at the beginning of the month, they have none of them. As they reach their income milestones, they check off one of their list. The one they check off, they can now indulge in. In this fashion, the rewards can serve their purpose without creating that void feeling we spoke of before. How does it work? Take your monthly income goal and divide it by the number of rewards you have on your list. For me like before, I have 6 things on my list, so my monthly income would be divided by 6. $4,000 ÷ 6 = $666.66. Add this number on top of itself 6 times, and write down each number as you do it. Make sure to write the numbers down in some form. You can even keep them in the notes section on your phone as we covered before.

Milestones

- $666.66

- $1333.32

- $1999.98

- $2666.64

- $3333.3

- $4000

For each milestone you hit, you unlock a reward of your choice. The same discipline that was mentioned in the emotional autopilot is the same here. For those activities that are getting you closer to your financial goals but are not currently producing money in that month, the process is similar to the one mentioned in the emotional autopilot. Use that stopwatch, and if you hit 10 hours, you unlock a reward. If you hit 20 hours, you get another reward. The reward unlocks can't go past 20 hours though. This is because you are rewarding your efforts, but you're not living in the future. If you find any of this to be a struggle, revisit chapter 3.

What if the monthly goal was not reached? Yes, the rewards list will need to take a hit. Remove one of the rewards you access to unlock, every time you don't hit your monthly goal. Remove them in order from least important to most important. Run the milestone drill with the different number and use the extra time to make more money. If you don't know how to make more money, revisit chapter 5. Hate to sound like a broken record but yes, discipline is the key. However, you have a stronger source to pull from here too. Ambition! These things you do to entertain yourself are nice, but are they more important than your financial goals? Think about this when you need a motivation boost. Emotional management works best for the king of the hill and builder personas.

For all the three ways of dealing with your emotions, if you are giving any amount of time to worthy causes or nonprofits, treat them like you treat activities that aren't producing immediate money results. Get that stopwatch out. Note that these charitable activities and the other activities are all in one bracket. For example, if I spend 5 hours volunteering at an event for a nonprofit and I spend 5 hours building a website for a new stream of income I'm starting, the total amount of hours would be 10 hours. We will call them reward hours. This means I would then be able to use those hours to contribute to the reward list. In what fashion will depend on which way you are using, emotional control, management, or autopilot. The reward hours still max out at 20 hours regardless of what percentage is coming from charitable activities or future money-making opportunities.

Paying bills

If you put 10 people in the same room and discuss how they each go about paying their bills, chances are you're going to get a lot of different responses. Even though we all have various bills, at the core, a bill is the same. It is something that needs to be paid with multiple ways to pay it. The thing is some of us favor specific methods over others. So, what makes up a way of paying a bill? Every way you can think of is one of or a blend of paying it directly or having it set on autopay. Out of this concept come to the three ways or techniques that we will cover here.

Technique one: Bill control

Some people at their core want to be in control of their financial situation at all times. To not be in control disturbs them. They picture things that could go wrong if they don't control all or most of the dynamics of their budget. Due to this, they learn all the elements of budgeting and forms of payment so that they are in control. This method is the most hands-on and involved way among the three techniques.

The way this person sees it, things may come, and they want to move things around in their budget. They want the freedom to do so. If the car payment was automatically paid via auto payment, they can't use it to address something that needed to be addressed. They would rather pay that bill late and use the money in the meantime to address that issue. This is an example of the type of control they must have. The person using this method is opposed to any type of automatic payment. If an automatic payment is cheaper than other methods, they will choose the alternative ways in a heartbeat. They feel they must have the ability to pay when THEY want to. This allows them the maximum flexibility over their budget, but it does mean they have to take time out of their day to actually make the payments. They have to call the phone number to pay their car note directly. They have to drive up to the bank to pay the mortgage. It requires both attention and time. That's the trade-off they have to make for that control. Control in exchange for time and focus put on the bill. If this is not a trade-off you want to make, one of the other techniques may work better for you. This is for those that embrace the ability to be in control of all the aspects of their bills. Bill control works excellent for the sniper and the conservative personas.

Technique two: Bill autopay

Do you not even want to be bothered about paying bills? Would you instead just take yourself out of the equation altogether? I'm sure you have better things you could be doing than paying bills and worrying about due dates. Some people consider this a wrong mentality to have. What's so bad about it? People that speak negatively about this are coming from a standpoint that something goes wrong. If you set it up the right way, it can't go wrong. If you answered yes to the previous questions asked, if you haven't already, you'll want to set up your bills on autopay.

The most autonomous way is to link your bank account if possible, and they can take the money out of your account on the bill due date. It's the opposite of bill control, and that is why you get the reverse here. You don't have to spend any time or attention on your bills because you've taken yourself out of the equation! Sure, bills get updated in some way now and then, so you'll have to make changes when that happens. The same goes for when you get new bills or pay off old ones. That doesn't happen every day though. For the most part, it's a hands-off process, but that comes at the cost of direct control. If you want to move things around and pay something late, since they have your bank info, they will sometimes take it out of your account unless it doesn't have enough money.

In some cases, if there isn't enough money, your bank could charge a fee. These cons come with this method, so they should be noted, but as I said, it's the method that requires the least amount of your time and attention. That time and care can be put in other places of your life like let's say ways to make more money! It's for those that want to focus on making more money and not on the dynamics of expenses but rather just ensuring they are taken care of. Bill autopay is ideal for the builder and the fame seeker.

Technique three: Bill Management

So, you can pay bills directly, or you can set it up on autopay, linking it to a bank account. What if you like the attributes of both though? You like the autonomous feel of something being charged without you having to do anything, and you also want control if, for whatever reason, you need to move things around. Does that not fit the definition of bill management? I'm not about to look up the meaning as I'm sure you follow me. Bill management here is a hybrid of autopay and bill control.

This is accomplished by setting up something that's autonomous and also something you have control over without fees involved. That's why you can't use your bank account here to fit this bill. If you wanted to halt on paying a bill for some reason, how much does a "stop payment" cost with your bank? Only you can answer that, but we both know it costs something. A great example of something that can be considered bill management is the billing institution having a debit card on file. That same debit card can be blocked on your end. It gives the desired effect of bill payment being autonomous without surrounding control. Even if you don't have a debit card you can block, you could move your money to the savings account or another bank.

Another example is the automatic mailing of checks. There are banks like chime and BB&T that will mail a check to a person or business, and this can be used to pay bills. It can sometimes be set up to get mailed out every month. This creates the same scenario as the debit card, which makes it fall under the bill management method.

To be clear, this isn't encouraging the dodging or the not paying of any bills. We all know that times come where something else in our lives is a higher priority than a bill. It's in those moments we choose to pay the bill later. The downside of this method is often; financial institutions are fully aware of the information presented in this bill section of this book and try to motivate people via incentive or fear to pay using their bank accounts. When I went to upgrade my phone plan and get a new phone, the sales representative told me my monthly bill would be $70 if I paid with my bank account. If not, it would be $80, a perfect example of an institution trying to incentivize me. Other times, to pay with your checking account is free while other forms of payment like online or phone charge fees named convenience, miscellaneous, etc. There are direct ways for using this bill control technique, such as paying at the institution or mailing a check, and they aren't fee heavy. Unfortunately, these fees are mainly found here, which would be the biggest con. With that being said, they can be minimized. Just make yourself aware of them, and you may be able to find ways around them. Bill management is good for the preserver and the king of the hill.

Our goals

When we think of goals, what comes to mind is our big overarching vision. While this is an example of a goal, what determines if something is a goal or not is what something is and not the scale of it. To dive into this deeper, what is the textbook definition of a goal? It's the object of a person's ambition or effort; an aim or desired result. This definition can fit something big or small. If you have in your budget an objective to spend a certain amount of money on something, that in itself is a goal. What's the best way to go about setting them, though? How specific should the goal be? How broad should it be? Just like the theme of this chapter, it depends on your personality. Below are 3 techniques that one can use to set goals in their budget to their advantage.

Technique one: Goal Control

This one seems a little strange, right? We all have goals in our budget for the 5/6 areas of finances. When those goals are very precise, and there are multiple in an area, that's when it reaches the goal control level. Where one person may budget for, let's say expenses and have that money set aside to be used in the month, the goal controller will have everything they will spend that month on expenses in the actual budget. They would have a budget like the following:

1. Donations to nonprofit: $60 to go towards the said nonprofit, $30 to a birthday gift for mom.

2. Expenses: Food: $280, Car note: $400, Mortgage: $1200, Cell phone bill: $80, Home internet: 100$.

3. Investments: Class on accounting payment plan: $110, Kimberly Clark stock purchase: $136, stock purchase of at&t: $32.44, real estate seminar: $300.

4. Self-spending: Hairdo: $120, dinner with a friend: $30, Netflix membership: $14.99, red dead redemption 2 video game: $60.

5. Savings: Roth IRA $500.

See a pattern here? It's very precise! There is nothing general about this budget. Everything is categorized within the 5/6 areas as it should be. In the areas are the very things that they will spend the money on. That's what I mean by goal control. Down to the penny, in every area is the exact thing that money will be spent on. This is because everything is in front of them. The greatest advantage of doing goals like this is that you are familiar with every aspect of your budget almost on the spot. Here, they flourish off of dissecting the 5/6 areas of the budget and putting every little thing in the budget under its name. These individual's details to the areas allow them to see an area as a combination of smaller tasks that money needs to be spent on. It gives them the ability to have a target-like approach to the budget. They spend money on one thing and then move on to the next. The next could be in the same area or a different one. Also, due to this being the case, if they need to make changes, they will be the quickest to do so. The downside is this again takes time and attention. It can also lead to being over-structured. The structure, focus, and detail can have a bleeding over effect into other areas of life that it may not be best suited in. The best example I can think of is relationships. When you see this happening, accept it for what it is and realize that you may need to loosen up some. Goal control makes the sniper and the conservative feel at home.

Technique two: Freeflow goals

Have you ever been at a place where you don't even think about spending money? When you see something you want, as long as you have the money, you get it. What brought about this circumstance may vary.

Maybe you got promoted at your job. Perhaps you just struck a deal with a client that will be a long and profitable relationship. Maybe the IPO of your business went well. Maybe sales, in general, have been consistent and easy lately. I could go on and on, but you get the point. Your emotions at this time were literally on autopilot. Of course, purchases that would cost most of your money would have some thought into them, but the smaller things, you just bought them.

Did you budget for what you bought though? Let me guess; your answer is yes and no. What do you mean? You mentally had money set aside to spend in that way. You might be thinking: "Spend in what way? What way could you possibly be referring to that we would all know?" Let's think. Could that way be one of the 5/6 areas? It would have to be, but you didn't have those stocks that you bought or that trip to six flags directly in the budget, did you? You just planned to spend a certain amount of money in that way and had the thought, feeling, or urge to spend it on that exact thing. There's nothing wrong with that. It's the opposite of goal control. You budgeted for the 5/6 areas, but you don't put exactly what you will spend money on in each area. You may not even know it yet. Why we most likely don't think about why we handle it like this is because we don't want life to be so rigid! We want it to be more on impulse. How would the same budget in the previous method of goal control look like here?

- Donation to be given: $90

- Expenses: $2,060

- Investments: $579

- Self-spending: $225

- Savings: $500

What's the difference? It's is all general! The money has been allocated to the 5/6 areas, but that's all that's in the budget. How the money is spent in each area is open. They may decide to go out bowling with a friend and take it out of the self area. They could be browsing the internet and come across a forex trading course for $300 and decide to take it out of their investments. Since it's so open, some things could fall in multiple areas, so if one area doesn't have enough, it could go in another one as long as it fits that area! For example, they see a Vitamix on Amazon for $349. That's going to allow them to make better recipes at home as well as healthier ones, which fall in the self area. There is not enough money, though! But if this can improve their health, they're getting a return on it down the road which makes it an investment too. That means that it can be taken out of the investment area. If they wanted, they could split the cost between the two areas. That would be a pain in the butt if everything were literally in the budget, but since it's not, it can be updated as you spend money. This method allows that type of freedom. On the same token, with that freedom can come a lack of focus. Make sure to stay in touch with what you want from all the areas and spend a decent amount of the money there before anywhere else. For example, if you want to improve your health, then a lot of your spending in the "self" financial area should be on things that can improve your health. Failure to have some kind of direction in your area will lead to you being too all over the place, and as a result, you may find that you're not moving forward in your overall goals. The freeflow style gets the fame seeker and the builder excited!

Technique three: Goal management

Have you ever felt that you don't want a budget that is too detailed? That makes life too rigid. At the same time, you don't want an over general budget. It's so vague that it makes you wonder if the budget is even serving its purpose. Why not blend the two? Make a budget that is not too general and not over-detailed. This is when the concept of goal management comes knocking on your door. Goal management is the art of making a budgeting method that gives you the structure, as well as the flexibility to spend without having to change the whole thing. This is done by putting the things you'll spend money on in the 5/6 areas in the budget but in broad categories. The result is it gives you the freedom to spend within a more flexible structure. How about we revisit the same budget we had for the previous two methods.

- Donations to nonprofits: $90

- Expenses: Food: $280, Car note: $400, Mortgage: $1200, Technology bills: $180

- Investments: Education: $410, Stocks: $169

- Self-spending: Myself: $120, Going out: $30, Streaming services: $15, Video games: $60

- Savings: $500 retirement account

Notice how it is similar to the goal control except that it's much broader. Some of the bills are combined into one category, like technology bills. Even those that aren't combined have been put in groups that others could fit in. Interestingly enough, this method eliminates the cons of the other two methods and also removes some of their pros. This method is not detailed enough to create the target-like sense of the goal control, and it's also not free to the point that it allows the same level of crossing among the areas when it comes to spending. What it does have going that neither of the other two has is it gives the budgeter a strong sense of direction without being too rigid in the details. The direction is not as strong as the goal control, but it's not stiff, which is considered a con to some. This works nicely for the king of the hill and the preserver.

Something to keep in mind is that these are recommendations based on the personality type. If you find that something sounds or seems better for you, then feel free to experiment. It is about finding what works best for you, meaning what delivers you convenience with and a sense of mental freedom. As you will see in the next chapter and phase, doing what works best for YOU, financial is the key to being successful financially.

You have now completed phase 4. Congratulate yourself, mainly because you're probably tired of me doing it. The next phase will take everything you have learned so far and present you with a way on how to see the inner workings of financial opportunities and decide if they are worth moving forward with or not. You can only see how opportunities can affect your earnings to spending ratio via the other phases only after you've gotten control over it. So many people every year pursue opportunities they would be better off leaving but waste precious time. Others ignore opportunities that would be perfect for them! Phase 5 will give you that x-ray vision mentioned in the beginning of this book. You will be able to see the factors that make the decision a thousand times easier and quicker once you do the formula enough times. It's the final and arguably most influential part of being a financially savvy person.

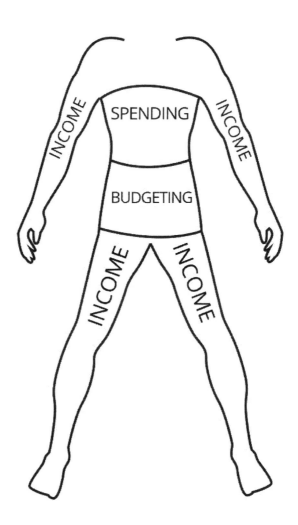

PHASE 5. EVALUATING OPPORTUNITIES

CHAPTER 11.

DEVELOPING FINANCIAL X RAY VISION:

HOW TO SPOT OPPORTUNITIES THAT ARE GOOD FOR

YOUR PERSONALITY AND GOALS

"Decide what you want, and then act as if it were impossible to fail."

Brian Tracy, Chairman and CEO of Brian Tracy International and author of over 40 books on finances.

How do you make Brain Tracy's quote a reality for yourself? You have to know REALLY what you want. In many ways, this is the ability that the whole book has been building up to. 10,000s of thousands of people a year are presented with opportunities to move them towards their financial goals. Without even noticing, this alone stresses a lot of them out because they want to move forward so that they can make the type of money wanted, but they don't know if it's right for them. How many people do you know that have moved forward with a financial opportunity only to find that it's not right for them? Maybe you have been one of them. Then they become frustrated that they wasted so much time in their life trying to make it work. The truth is, if you don't know how much money you want to make, what type of income you want, how you want that money to be made, how to budget that money, and how to tell if making money that way falls within your personality, you run the risk of being disappointed. Throughout your journey to build your financial person, you have learned how to do all these things separately. While they play a significant role by themselves, they are vital when it comes to evaluating financial opportunities. Before gaining the skill of assessing things in the financial world, you have to see your role in it first.

What is your natal personality?

Out of the 6 financial personas that we've covered, which one are you? This is a question you have most likely had since you finished chapter 8. Some of you instinctively know which one you are. Others may be wondering as they may see some of themselves in more than one. Some of you may be wondering how that is even possible. Don't worry, like usual, we will address these and many more questions. What will be referred to as your natal financial personality is the one of the six personas that you are from birth. Just say it. "What do you mean? I wasn't handling money when I was a child." Unless you played house a lot, I see where you're coming from.

This is the persona that has the tendencies that you have had since you first started getting involved with money. These are personality traits, and you are born with them. They show themselves, both the positive and negative attributes when you enter the financial world. For example, if your natal personality is the king of the hill, you find that you always had to spend money on investments

249

and expenses. If it's the builder, you were always fascinated by financial formulas and tended to prioritize savings and investments. If it's the fame seeker, you always ended up using your talents to make money and invariably spend the most on yourself and investments. If it's the sniper, you found that you were regularly explosive when it comes to money and your money mostly went to savings and expenses. You exhibited the positive and negative traits of that persona from the start as well.

It is vital that you know which one you are because that is your power zone in the financial world. I was told when I was 21 by a wise elder that money and career should be the area you encounter the least resistance in when moving forward in life. You should be using what comes naturally to you to generate money. So many people struggle financially because of this simple fact. If you are still unsure which one you are, here are some questions you can ask yourself to shine clarity on the topic. If you've had a period in your life where money wasn't tight, what two areas did you spend money on every month? Expenses, self-spending, investments or savings? We adapt based on our circumstances, but if there aren't any hard ones going on, chances are what you are spending money on is simply, what emotionally charges you. Which persona, in general, sounded the most like you? What special ability seems like something you would do or have leveraged before? Which person keeps popping up as the answer to these questions? Asking yourself these questions should help you determine which one is your natal. Once you do this, you will be much better equipped to get what you need from the financial marketplace.

What persona do you desire to develop?

Your natal personality should like I said before, be your powerhouse. You may have felt a drawing toward another persona, though. Like it sounded cool, and you want to be that persona. Being honest with yourself, you know that's not you though, or at least not entirely. We all have a natal personality and a personality that we seek to develop. Sometimes, we know not why though. We just do. It could be that you saw people around you with this personality type and you wanted to develop into it. It could be the expectations society puts on you. It could really be anything. The important thing is that you know which one it is. It is also important to realize that the persona you desire to develop is not your natal personality. This means that you don't have the talent of that persona to do things like them. For example, the king of the hill has in his persona to work with others to achieve a financial result. That is something that someone whose natal personality is the conservative would find challenging to do since she is very introverted. On the other side of the coin, the conservative can delay gratification and work until it pays off financially. That is something the king of the hill would find emotionally challenging since he is a very active person with the expectation of knowing when something will pay off. Desiring to develop a persona means that you want to achieve the good things that persona will bring but lack the natural talent to do so.

In other words, you will have to work to develop the skills and traits of that persona. Great wealth is often achieved when the persona someone wants to develop is the same as their natal personality. This manifests as the desire to use and refine one's talents of that persona. This person easily achieves a loop of work and talent. They don't have to develop anything since they have the talent. All they need is just to refine those talents, and since it's their natal, they also enjoy it. That doesn't mean that if you desire to develop another persona, you can't achieve great wealth. It does mean that you have to be honest with yourself about the situation. You seek to develop that which does not come naturally to you. That's why your natal is your power zone. At least, 70% of your income should come from the income stream type that fits your natal. From there, you can develop the persona you desire without the financial duress of having to make quick money from it.

Some questions that will help you find your developmental persona: Which one simply stood out to you? Which one did you picture yourself doing but you haven't done anything like it before? Which one just straight up sounds appealing to you? Which one, when you read the description of it, seemed cool? You borderline envy those characteristics. You are wanting to be and have them. The persona that keeps popping up as the answer here is the one you seek to develop. Since it may help you to find both your natal and developmental personas, I will share with you my experience with all 6 personas so that it may help you in finding these two things.

My story with the 6 personas

At a young age, I always pictured a life where I didn't have to worry about money. Your thoughts are, "What makes you so unique?" If I had it my way when I was little, I would have money coming in my whole life while I sit back and play video games. Such is the viewpoint of a naive child at this point, though. As I got older, what I wanted morphed into wanting to just do my part without having to deal with the day to day of things. Without realizing it, what I wanted was to work now and receive the benefits in the future. This effectively eliminated the sense of urgency of money for me. I didn't know how I would obtain this. I just knew this was what I wanted. What I wanted was OP or steady passive income. I also, from a young age, always saved money. Even when I was just in elementary, I saved up my allowance and asked my mom if I could switch out my smaller bills for a $100 bill. I did this because I knew I wouldn't want to break it. She did, and I held that $100 for a year until my mom stopped buying me video games, and I had to start buying them myself. From time to time, my mom asked if she could borrow the $100 bill and gave it back at the end of the week!

Whenever I wanted something, saving money was not an obstacle for me. In high school, I got an allowance of $50 every two weeks. I didn't buy anything that I didn't have to and saved $600 for over 4 months to buy a PS3. The financial area of savings came naturally to me, and it was just part of my personality. I found myself ignore spending money on myself so that I could save for what I wanted or needed down the road. I got the PS3 to play video games with, but then, I met someone on the PlayStation network that showed me how to use my PS3 to do other things. The PS3 can function as a computer if you know how to set it up. I won't bore you with all the techno details, but what was most useful for me was I started using it to watch YouTube and surf the internet. Of course, I would be looking up the things that any teenage boy would lookup. I'll let your imagination fill in the blanks, but I also would just be searching for random ways to make money. Some of those ways that I found back then, I still use it to make money today.

It finally occurred to me that I had bought something that was giving me value in return. By the definition set in this book, this was also an investment. In addition to this, I was always fascinated by the cycle of things. How things go up and down as well as things that produce results consistently. Eventually, this led me to learn about real estate and stocks. I shied away from them because I had not been exposed to them, and I knew little to nothing about them.

According to everything I have said so far, looking at it is implies that my natal financial personality was the builder even though I didn't know it at the time. I then started following people in the network marketing field. It was offering a type of passive income, and that seemed great since I wanted passive income. The kind of people I saw and wanted to be like were the king of the hills. At this point in my life, I was shy and reserved. Needless to say, that didn't go anywhere. When I was older, I had come out of my shell and had more ambition and was looking to get involved in business. Someone I knew told me that if I wanted to get involved in business, I must learn how to sell and network marketing is an excellent place to develop those skills. He then referred me to one of his colleagues.

As I sat in one of the conventions, I started to lose interest. I didn't like how the company had control over the prices, commissions paid, and promotions. At that point, I decided that I wanted to start my own business. A few months later, I started what would be my first business Indigenous remedies, known by its kibantu name as Asili Tiba. I sold herbal teas and capsules, and here began my journey of being in the sniper persona. I learned how to sell and how to run a business more or less through self-education. I designed the website, answered phone calls, ran promotions, and inventory. I have a mom with a bachelor's degree in business, an aunt with her own janitorial company and a personal trainer who had his own business that I talked to on the regular. I had people to talk to when I was unsure about things sometimes, but most of the time, I preferred to figure things out on my own.

The business was part-time, and then I entered the workforce when things got slow. About a year later, I started working for Amazon as a seasonal associate, and things began increasing in the business. The business was very good, but it couldn't be sustained. I loved the potential for financial independence it gave me. I could have quit Amazon and gone full time and been great, but I realized that I was getting further away from what I wanted when I was younger, which was passive income. I then had a week of self-reflection and decided to shut the business down.

After this, Amazon peak was here, and it was 45 to 60 hours shifts with overtime in there. Funny enough, the transmission in my car went out right before peak time at Amazon, so I had to get a ride to work for the majority of peak season. I knew how much a new transmission would cost, and I could make the money. The sniper locked his weapon, aimed at his target and shot. Peak ended, I bought a new transmission, and things were fine for about two months, then everything you could imagine started going wrong with the car. Eventually, it wasn't drivable. The car was paid for, and I didn't want to finance a car and have another monthly expense, a car note. Regardless of what I wanted at the time, that was the only option. Since I needed a reliable way to get to work, I took out two payday loans to help with the downpayment for a brand new car. With a new car, I could now get to Amazon.

I was then converted into a permanent associate, but with peak over, hours drop down to part-time. I needed more money if I was going to pay off the payday loans I took out. This was when I started working at Whole Foods Market part-time. From 5.00 am to noon, I would work at Whole Foods. After a small break, from 2:30 pm to 6:30 pm (7:30 pm if they flexed up), I worked at Amazon. Most days in between time, I picked one of my friends who also worked at

Amazon up from her apartment after my Whole Foods shift and took her back to her apartment on the way home. All of this was challenging but there was a part of me that genuinely enjoyed the thrill of the challenge. That was the sniper persona that had been fully developed. I remained in the sniper persona for a few months until the payday loans were paid off and things lightened up.

It was during this time that my spending shifted from savings and expenses to self-spending and expenses. Since I had two jobs, always getting somewhere between 45 and 64 hours combined from both of them left me with excessive cash every month. At this point, I gradually started taking on the preserver persona. I had passion for getting a high position at either Amazon or Whole Foods, and since I just came out of a debt situation, I had the idea of preserving my current debt-free lifestyle and the luxury of being able to buy what I wanted within reason due to the extra money. Seeing how the builder and the sniper are on the lower end of the spectrum when measuring them in terms of emotions, it was very different being in this persona. I didn't know exactly what I wanted to do with my life financially at this time. I just knew I wanted to make more money with less of my time.

With peak at Amazon about a month and some change away, I quit working at Whole Foods when it was clear that there weren't going to be any chances to move up. I knew when peak time rolled around again that it would be time to hit it hard again. Here, I learned an interesting lesson. I expected my mind and emotions to enter the sniper persona again but they didn't. Instead, I held on the preserver persona. Thinking back now, I now know that I didn't enter the sniper persona simply because the circumstances didn't demand it. On top of this, my spending was still expenses first and self-spending second, which are the preserver's strengths.

I did everything I needed to learn the protocols of amazon's operations and worked hard. I wanted to become a PA or a process assistant. They were the people that were between the regular associates and management. They got paid more and played a role in the running of the shift. It paid off, and when another building opened after peak, I applied and got the PA position. I was now making the same money I was making when I was working 60 hours at Whole Foods and Amazon. I just worked an average of 40 hours with occasional overtime, and it was in one place instead of two.

Things were good for a while, but I started to fill a void inside of me. I still had the ambition to make money differently. I craved passive income so I could be free to pursue what I wanted. What was happening was that I was feeling the desire for the persona that I wanted to be, which was the builder. This is why it's crucial to go ahead and pursue the persona you desire to become. If you don't, there will always be a void in your life that you will start seeking to fill in other ways.

About a year later, I decided to quit and once again enter the world of self-employment. I didn't want to start another business like my first one though. I knew I wouldn't be satisfied unless I had a business that truly had the potential to provide passive income. That's when I signed up with a network marketing company that offered health and wellness products, which was another passion of mine. It was during this period that I developed the fame seeker persona. I had learned the skills on how to sell from already, having started a business before. On top of this, my upline, which was the personal trainer I spoke of before gave me a solid system of how to give an assessment as well as a formula for talking to customers. I was giving assessments and selling products. My sales closing rate was consistently 90% or higher, and I loved it. The void I spoke of went away for a small while but eventually returned. The money was great, but it's UA or unsteady active income. This means how much I made was determined by how hard I worked, which I loved, but it wasn't the OP income I was desiring.

My upline said that I was good at sales, but if I desired passive income, it was time to start recruiting. I did start recruiting, and I got people signed up, and I had a downline of my own for a while. Something started happening that I didn't like though. In network marketing, if your downline doesn't perform, your passive income stops or decreases. I found myself having to motivate others to make money, which was something I found I didn't like. For a while, even I wasn't sure why I didn't. I've always been a social person, and I have motivated people to change their lives in other areas like health, friendships, and lifestyle. After doing what some would consider soul searching, I found out that I didn't like motivating people to make money because it was not the process I went through. Those other areas I mentioned were areas that I had help in and changed too. I was simply duplicating what someone had done for me before, which I enjoyed. Money was different, though. Don't get me wrong, I had help along the way, but I was always self-motivated in this area. I wanted what I wanted when it came to financial goals, and I put the work in and got the result I was seeking.

I would often get frustrated when I would sign someone up, and they wouldn't start making money. They needed motivational support, and that was something that I, at the time, couldn't give. Since that was not my process financially, I didn't value it enough to give it. My upline told me that I needed to start looking for people like myself to recruit. Those who were self-motivated and just needed a system to put energy into the opportunity. The amount of work that would take was something I didn't deem worth it to commit to. With my desire to make sales in this way steadily dropping, I decided to start doing Uber and UberEats on the side to supplement my sales income. I kept doing my sales for a little while, but I eventually stopped because it wasn't getting me closer to what I desired.

Soon after, I was on YouTube researching things about being an Uber driver. I saw various channels that were talking about the money they make off of Uber referrals. I felt a spark inside of me. All they were doing was teaching about how to be successful as an Uber driver via strategies. It was nothing that I couldn't duplicate. I noticed that no one was doing it for Ubereats. That's when I finally entered my natal personality and the one I desired to be, the builder. I mastered the art of being an UberEats driver and made videos and a course on how to on YouTube. While doing this, I started receiving referral money from those that signed up using my code. I did not have to motivate them because the concept of making money from their phones attracted self-motivated people. I didn't have to physically teach or coach them because the course and the videos were answering their questions. My cashflow did not demand me to do work currently today for the money to come in. It was truly passive. With that undertaking being successful, I decided to pursue YouTube monetization. This was successful and was yet another passive income stream since the course and videos I had made were now making YouTube money. The void simply vanished. I hadn't reached my income goals mentioned earlier in this book, but I was making money that was in line with my natal personality and the persona that I was desiring to be. All I had to do was to repeat the formula with whatever I wanted, which I both enjoyed and was craving. My income couldn't help but increase.

Towards the end of that year, I had enough passive streams setup that I took a month off to go on a raw foods vegan diet and detox my body. During this time, I also used this as a mental reset, and I didn't work any. It was something

I always wanted to do at the end of every year as a reboot to go into the next year strong. Before, I couldn't because I didn't have the income or time. That wasn't the case now. This was when I carried the persona of the conservative. My YouTube revenue was still relatively small since I had just got the app lifestyle monetized. My primary income was Uber and UberEats referrals, which was UP or unsteady passive income. This is the income that works best with the conservative.

I then experienced something which I considered crazy. The void which I assumed was coming did not return. I wondered why? It finally hit me that the emptiness didn't come back because the persona I had desired to be had already been fulfilled. Yes, I had a different persona, but the skills I used to generate the income of that persona, as well as the mindset, didn't go anywhere. I could jump back into it anytime I wanted to, and I knew I could. This filled the void. This is why it is so key to develop that persona desire but have your natal personality support it in the meantime.

When the new year came, I knew that it was time. These ideas and the financial systems I had developed; it was time to make them public. They had been inside my head long enough. So many people struggle financially because they don't have a way to think when it comes to the financial world. I had found my mission statement. The key was to find a way to do this and monetize it in a way that would bring me OP income, which is the income that my natal personality, the builder, works best with. Immediately, as if the idea was shot into my head, I asked myself, "Why not write a book." It can teach people a new way of navigating the financial world, and it could reach more people than I ever could if physically teaching. I knew to get this offer the ground in the timeframe

I wanted would require me to adapt to another persona. That being the persona of the king of the hill.

It was then that I become the king of the hill. I was in the first stage, the solo one who stays on top of his own life. I started raising money for the project, researching what it would take not only to publish it but make it available in all forms. Those forms being paperback, ebook, and audiobook. Each month, I had a different task to do, which cost money. This put the top two areas of my spending on my financial statement investments and expenses. Both of which are the king of the hill's strengths. I did this somewhat on purpose because I knew it would help in fully developing this persona.

Towards the end of writing the rough draft for this book, I noticed something going on around me. I had the financial task of raising the money to produce this book. Most people around me had a different type of financial problem. Almost everyone I knew, both family and friends, start having financial problems. I started feeling responsible to help them financially. Not in the way of giving them money but rather giving them some kind of opportunity. I had a friend who fell on hard times, and his car was giving him trouble. I couldn't even tell him to hop on Ubereats. I started thinking about how I could help someone in that situation. It was here when I began entering the king of the hill stage 2. Just like the idea of writing this book, another thought hit me. What if I could create an affiliate program after the book is launched for those who want to tell others about it? This could help anyone in any circumstance since the book can be an ebook or audiobook. That means they would have no overhead cost. On top of this, it can make any of the 4 types of income. That means that regardless of their personality type, it could help them. Like a true king of the hill, if my team succeed, I will succeed! The thought went from an idea to a vision, then to reality.

I share my experiences with the 6 personas not to brag but to emphasize the importance of making money with both your natal personality and the persona you seek to develop. We all have one we desire and one we are born with. It is finding the right way for you to combine the two that result in both financial success and emotional fulfillment. This, in turn, makes the prospect of great wealth possible.

Anyone can succeed, given the right environment

Realizing your personality type is vital to success in the financial world. When evaluating a financial opportunity, it should serve as the foundation for your decision. As you will learn later in this chapter, a person's natal personality can determine if something is even worth your effort or not. The truth is you can make anything work. The degree to which you make it work depends on the balance between your natural talent, which is the attributes of your natal personality or the amount of effort you put in to develop the traits needed for the opportunity. The more something requires things outside of your personality, the more effort you have to put in. To demonstrate this, I created a short story that illustrates exactly how this works.

A long time ago, back when humanity was still starting civilization, there were four tribes. For demonstration purposes, we will call each tribe a letter. Each one had their own way of thinking when it came to how to make money and in what ways they valued it. Tribes A and B loved working hard in order to make a lot of money. The concept of working today and not get paid until the future came was straight-up strange to them and they did not like it. In other words, they liked active income. The other two tribes, C and D, didn't like the pressure of having to work hard all at once to make money. They were happy with working a slow pace and getting paid in the future. These two tribes liked passive income. If this wasn't enough difference here, they also disagreed on the method of how they should get paid. Tribes A and C like the idea of steady income for work while B and D didn't like their income being limited at a set rate. They wanted to have the sky be the limit. Tribes A and C wanted steady income. Income that came in at a constant rate for their continued efforts. Tribes B and D wanted unsteady income. Income that depended on how much work they put in at any given time. The tribes bumped heads with each other when it came to matters of commerce. Always not meeting each other expectations.

Finally, the heads of each tribe went to see the village elder. After listening to all four of their sides, he said that if they want to find any kind of cohesion, they needed to break off from each other and start separate villages. The four leaders agreed and started their own communities. The tribe that liked orthodox or steady active income became the village of OA. The tribe that wanted unorthodox or unsteady active income became known as the village of UA. The tribe that loved Orthodox or steady passive income was the village of OP. The tribe that valued unorthodox or unsteady passive income inherited the title of the village of UP. Out of these four villages were born the 6 personas of the financial world.

Each person was born in one of the four villages. Growing up there, they saw how money was earned and valued the earning of it in that way. When they grew up and when it came to making money in the way that was done in their village, it was easy. It was a part of them. It was intuitive to them because they had seen it their whole lives. If they traveled to one of the other four villages, they would not be able to make money as easily. The method of making money in that village was somewhat foreign to them. Sometimes, they would even have trouble with it. It didn't take them long to realize that they had the highest chance for financial success if they were in their own village where making money was easy due to them using the talent and skills they were familiar with to do so. This was the income stream type that was in line with that persona's personality. They were covered in chapter 8, but they will be listed here again just to save you the trouble of flipping a few pages.

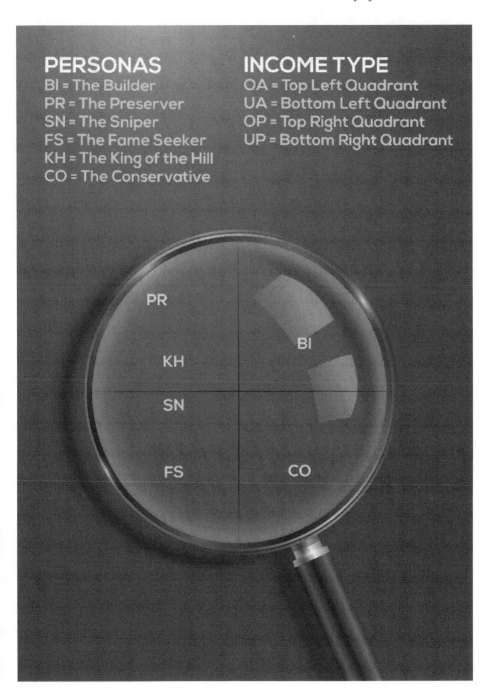

PERSONAS
BI = The Builder
PR = The Preserver
SN = The Sniper
FS = The Fame Seeker
KH = The King of the Hill
CO = The Conservative

INCOME TYPE
OA = Top Left Quadrant
UA = Bottom Left Quadrant
OP = Top Right Quadrant
UP = Bottom Right Quadrant

PR

BI

KH

SN

FS

CO

1. The builder: OP (Steady passive income)

2. The preserver: OA (Steady active income)

3. The sniper: UA (Unsteady active income)

4. The fame seeker: UA (Unsteady active income)

5. The king of the hill: OA (Steady active income)

6. The conservative: UP (Unsteady passive income)

The diagram shows the money magnifier with the 6 personas inside of it.

A persona's best chance for financial success is to stick to their village. Anyone can develop the skills to be successful in another town, but it will take more work since it is not what clicks for them emotionally. With that being said, does that mean it is not possible? Hardly. Remember what I said before about not neglecting the persona you desire to develop. What would you do if that persona has a different type of income stream strength? Do you just say screw it and forget about it? That's why the natal personality should be the power zone. So, you can go and put in the work to develop another one if you so desire without the immediate financial duress.

It is also important to note that even though another village would feel foreign, the sharing of a certain value with their own village makes it easier to learn their ways or that type of stream of income. If you recall, both tribes A and B valued activity when it comes to income. That means that if members of each other's tribes find themselves in the other's village, yes, it would be strange but they would emotionally recognize that value and that would make it easier to learn their ways. For example, the preserver would be in the village of OA or orthodox active income. If she found herself in the village of UA or Unorthdox active income, yes, the unsteady nature of it would be foreign, but she is used to actively working for money now to get cash immediately. If she could adapt to the unsteady characteristics, she will find success. If she was in the village of UP, she might be in trouble because income there is utterly foreign to her. It's unsteady and passive, which is against everything she knows and emotionally responses to. Could she make it work? Yes, but it's going to take a hell of a lot of work. Why do that when you can just use your talents to make money in your village and enjoy it? What if she had the desire to be a conservative though and she was already successful in her home village of OA income. It would be work to develop the UP income she desires, but she wouldn't have to do so under financial pressure. She can just go back home when needed while generating the UP income. Now be honest, if you had this perspective before looking at an opportunity and you knew what type of income it can give you, would this not take a lot of duress out of the decision of doing it or not?

Neighbors rub off on each other

Continuing with our village story, you'll notice that some personas inside the Money Magnifier are very close to the cusp that separates the incomes. A good example of this would be the king of the hill and the sniper. When a persona is close to the cusp, in the village metaphor, they are near the border that separates the villages; the villages aren't at war with each other. They are free to come and go as they please. This lead to many children having friends that were also close to the cusp in the other village. They would tell stories to each other about how their older relatives are making money. At first, they sounded strange to each other, but after hearing enough of them, they became familiar with their ways and started to respect them. Once they grow up, they still have vivid memories of the stories and scenarios their childhood friends would tell them. Some of them are still friends. These are the people that they could cross over to the other village and it wouldn't be too foreign to them since they lived on the cusp. Applying that to the money magnifier, the king of the hill's income home is OA income, but he is so close to the cusp between OA and UA that he could cross over to UA and be more or less okay. The same applies to the sniper. UA is his natal but being so close to the cusp, he could cross over to the OA and be fine. It goes both ways, though. If a persona is far from the cusp of their neighboring village, their methods are even more foreign, and it will take more work to learn their ways and start responding emotionally. The conservative is pretty far into the UP, and even though UA is the neighbor, it is still far for the conservative. Going over there can be done, but it would take more work than it would for let's say the sniper to go to the OA. These are the things that you want to consider when looking for your main source of income or a second source.

Taxes: What will they be like?

Putting our imaginations back aside, the tax ramifications of making money certain ways need to be thought about also when looking at an opportunity. A lot of people skip this step, but what is the point of making a bunch of money with the said opportunities only to lose a good chunk of it to taxes? Taxes are our biggest expense, and since that is the case, you need to know all you can about what it will be like if you start making considerable money with the opportunity in question. Keep in mind that you should always seek the advice of a CPA or tax professional if in doubt. I am not a tax advisor, but I will share some general information that is good to know. Also, keep in mind that the vocabulary used will switch from what I have been using to tax chagrin.

There are three types of income as far as the IRS is concerned. Ordinary earned income, portfolio income, and passive income. Ordinary earned income, also known as active income, is considered money you work for. It is the highest taxed income amount out of the three. The amount of taxable income will vary from person to person. To find out what tax bracket you fall in based on your income, google "IRS tax brackets (put the current year here)." It will pop up on various government websites. Portfolio income is income made from stocks in the forms of interest, dividends, or capital gains. If the opportunity you're looking at has this income, will it be short term capital gains or long term? Short term capital gains are treated as ordinary income. This is an important question to ask yourself. Passive income is income that comes from royalties or real estate rental income. It is the least taxed among the three. Keep in mind that these IRS definitions are not to be confused with active and passive income in the context of the money magnifier. Remember, I'm using the tax charging briefly while covering this tax section.

Which of the three incomes will the opportunity produce for you? Will it provide more than one? We can't forget about the deductions that can be utilized for CERTAIN ways of making money. How many deductions can be taken advantage of in the said opportunity? One of the reasons I found Uber and Ubereats to be appealing is because I could use the standard mileage deduction, which at the time was for every mile I drove, I was allowed a 54 cent deduction. This, in combination with other things, lead to me paying zero dollars in taxes that year. Does the opportunity even offer the ability to take deductions? Out of the five ways of making money, which is it? As an employee, entrepreneur, contractor, investor, or referrer/affiliate?

All of these things that we have covered in this chapter. Your personality, the income stream, the taxes, the type of way of earning, it all boils down to the formula that I'm about to reveal to you. This is the formula that will allow you to evaluate a financial opportunity and decide to move forward or decline without any feelings of regret or uncertainty.

Opportunity evaluation formula

When evaluating a financial opportunity, write down six words vertically: Income, method, effort, time, fun, stress. Confirm what type of income it will bring you. If it is said to bring you multiple streams, only count the biggest one. Does this opportunity offer the type of income that your personality is biased toward (OA, UA, OP, UP)? Then look at the type of skills that will be needed to make it an effective source of income. Next, determine if the skill(s) are within your talents. This means that you already have the skill(s) developed or you have a natural talent towards it, so cultivating it won't be too difficult.

Next, are you earning money as an employee, entrepreneur, contractor, investor, or referrer/affiliate? Write it down next to the method. Have an idea of which one you want to earn money as. With that in mind, give the effort it will take to make this opportunity a meaningful contributor to your income on a scale of 1 to 10. Keep in mind the following questions: Do I have the skills for this? If not, what skills will I need to learn? Is training on those skills available, or will I need to acquire them on my own? When using these skills, do I feel great or very stressed?

Based on if you have the skills or not, what is the estimated time frame you can expect to start making the desired income? Some questions to keep in mind:

How long will it take me to learn those skills? What type of money will I earn along the way while working to reach my desired income?

After this, rate how much fun you can see yourself having doing this or getting involved and rate this on a scale of 1 to 10. Ask yourself questions such as: When doing this, do I find it fun? Is it invigorating when I achieve a milestone on the way to my goal of doing this? Will I meet great and like-minded people doing this? Can I use the skills I learn here to improve in other areas of life? Can these skills I learn be used to make money in similar or different ways?

The final step is to rate the amount of stress you feel doing this on a scale of 1 to 10. This should be a combination of how you feel when it is presented to you as well as when you are doing the work itself. Questions to ask: Does my dread for this outweigh the fun of doing it? Did my energy increase when it was presented to me or decrease? Does thinking about this inhibit my ability to relax? It is important to note that the fun and stress levels change once you actually start. Generally, you will see a continuation of doing an activity will slowly remove the stress from it as well as raise the level of joy generated from doing it. However, when there are so many ways to make money out there, why not pick one that you enjoy right off the bat? Only you can decide that.

We are now going to score the opportunity based on the factors and questions we've covered.

If the persona you see having success is your natal personality, add 5 points.

Is the method for making money here what you want? If not, subtract 5 points.

Effort: If you have the skills, add 10 points. If you have some of the skills, add 7points. If you don't have the skills, but you have talent in the field that hasn't been exploited yet, add 3 points. If you don't have any skills or talent in that field, add no points.

What is the time frame you want to make this income in? This is in general, regardless of this particular opportunity. Once you answer this question, match it up against the expected time frame for the opportunity. If they match up well, gain 5 points. If it falls a little short of your expectations, earn no points. If there is a big gap between them (months or even a year), minus 5 points.

What number did you give the fun? Add that amount points.

What number did you give the stress? Minus that amount of points?

Should you move forward with the opportunity?

Between 35 and 28: It seems like this was made for you! There is great wealth in this opportunity for you if you decide to move forward. All this comes while you're having fun. It's literally getting paid for doing something you like to do.

Between 27 and 21: The pros of this opportunity outweigh the cons. While there may be stress and time frames that make you hesitant to move forward, the thrill of its fun nature and the usefulness of the skill(s) combined with the desire for the income will eventually reduce the stress and the frustration of the lack of immediate results based on your time frames. Cultivate the ability to delay immediate gratification, and there will be success.

Between 20 and 14: Skills must be cultivated under stressful conditions. The reward of the income is there, but it is buried underneath unreasonable expectations. Having high expectations isn't necessarily bad, but it is not balanced with the joy of achieving the income and acquiring new skills and having fun along the way. Moving forward is not recommended unless this opportunity will make you develop skills that you see you MUST have to move forward in life.

Under 13: One does not have the skills required to reach the desired income within a reasonable time frame. Frustration based on stress and/or time frames will follow. With so many different types of ways to make money in today's society, it wouldn't make any sense to move forward.

This formula may take you a while to do, being your first time evaluating an opportunity, but each time you do it, it will get both faster and easier. The main reason people move forward when they should not and don't move forward when they should is simply a lack of self-awareness and the correct valuation of the opportunity. This gives you the ability to be self-aware by knowing your strengths based on your natal personality, and its best income as well as measuring the amount of time you're willing to commit vs. the amount of effort you're willing to put in. This allows you to see what the opportunity has to offer you in its entirety. Of course, this has no use to you if you don't use it. That's why the next assignment below exists.

Final Assignment of the book

Using this formula for evaluating a financial opportunity, look up 10 to 20 ways of making money. Specifically, look for ones that seem like it might be a good fit for you as well as ones you know are not. Use this formula to come up with a final number. Check to see where your number fits in the formula and if it is recommended that you move forward or not. Find articles about it. Look up the opportunity on YouTube and listen to what others have to say about it. If you can, find someone who is already doing it and ask them questions. Put on your detective hat and investigate! If you can't figure out something in the formula that you need, like "what type of income is it or the method the money is made," keep searching until you can fill that blank. This is like a muscle. The more you use it, the stronger your sense of self-awareness and valuing opportunities will be. Not only will this get practice under your belt, but you may find yourself with a few opportunities that are good for you. Then you can decide if you want to use one of the opportunities to make money with.

This chapter has been about the ability to evaluate a financial opportunity effectively, whether it is presented to you or you run across it on your own. If you ever find yourself getting rusty in this area, doing the assignment above regularly, especially when you are looking to increase your income, is highly recommended.

In summary, you have completed phase 5, and in doing so, you now have the x-ray vision to spot financial opportunities that are best for you. This seals the completion of your journey on developing your financial person. A celebration should be in order! Seriously, you should reward yourself in some means. Doing the assignments with the systems given in each phase, you have become a different person: a more financially savvy person. Not only can you get your own earning to spending ratio in control, but from here on out, any financial books you read in the future now have a place to fall in your life.

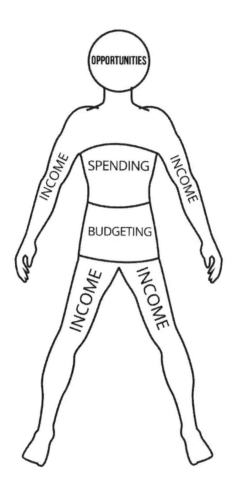

Times may change, and we must adapt to the new tools and information they bring with it. Each phase in this book has focused on this, but as a summary, I will cover the systems that will now and will forever bring you power in the financial world. I say that with confidence because these systems are built off of human nature, and we both know that will never change.

Income: The Money Magnifier will allow you to identify the type of income you are working for that you want in the future. This, in turn, gives you the ability to see the income type you want and work on the characteristics that are required to make it rain in that stream. As your ability to make more of the kind of money you want increases, you can always revisit the assignments in chapter 3 "the will to increase income." You'll have the capability to make more $$$, which means what you can achieve financially will be higher.

Budget: Knowing the 5/6 areas of finances and the roles they play in your life gives you a boarder perspective on budgeting. More importantly, the formulas you've learned can be used to provide you feedback on what areas of your financial life are neglected and which ones are on full display. From there, you can even find out the equation to make sure all areas are receiving attention, and likewise serving their purpose.

Spending: We all have our spending habits, and they produce both pros and cons. In identifying which of the 6 personas you are, you can be aware of the drawbacks that come with that persona and work on them. At the same time, you can capitalize on your strengths.

Opportunities: As the constructing of your financial person was nearly finished, you made the final push by learning the evaluation formula. With this formula under your belt, you can confidently seek out opportunities to make more money or evaluate the ones that come to you. It gets you to your decision without the ambiguity. You know why you want to move forward or not because you can see if it fits both you and your agenda.

As Neo K Marcellus, Author of the self-development book series; The tao of becoming a lady or gentleman of letter says, "Our outcomes are directly related to our inputs." The amount of input you put in these systems will equal the output they give to you. The more you use these financial methods, the more results you will see and the easier it will get. The good news is all of them are based on universal financial factors, so the need for them will never diminish. At the same time, you will find that there is no shortage of opportunities to use them.

Thank you for reading this book and building your financial person. If you found value in this book, would ask that you leave a honest review on amazon or a <u>rating</u> on the website. It helps further get this information out to those who need it. If you would also like to more directly contribute to getting this book out, I encourage you to apply for my affiliate program. You can earn up to 50% commission on book sales and up to 25% on non book products. Just visit the website below to get started.

Although you've laid the strong financial foundation, the next step is to plant some seeds in it that produces money trees for you. If you want to learn about some of those seeds, I encourage you to go to my website at <u>www.financialanatomy.net</u> or visit the financial anatomy YouTube channel. There, you will find tons of free content to help you in reaching your $$$ goals. You will also find not just me but others who are on the same financial journey as you. Whether we realize it or not, we start our financial lives living behind a wall, not seeing our true potential. It is society's responsibility to bring that potential out and break that wall. Only once the wall is broken, do we see the life of abundance that was always there, we just couldn't see. While society, in general, is not bringing that potential out, we have the capability to do it ourselves and with it comes the world of abundance that we knew was out there but didn't know how to get to it. That's no longer the case for you, is it? I'll see you on the other side.

Go out there and take control of your financial destiny!

ABOUT THE AUTHOR

Elijah is the creator of The App Lifestyle and The Anatomy Of Financ ial Success series. He has also made several free youtube videos on money management and how to make money from your phone. Through his books and training videos, he has helped 100s of people both make more money and manage it once they have it. After entering the world of business in 2012 at the age of 20, Elijah had to quickly learn the tricks of the trade when it came to finances. Since then, he has gotten involved in various  endeavors involving money such as working for Whole Foods Market, being a PA (Process Assistant) at Amazon, networking marketing and making money online. Throughout all of these undertakings, he saw the universal themes that ensured financial success in all of these and developed a system to manage those themes. He is truly appalled at how being financially successful is not taught at the high school level so that students are effectively prepared for the real world. Due to this, it is his mission to share the financial systems that have made him successful with those (especially young adults) that feel they can't achieve their financial goals due to fear, lack of motivation or not knowing how.

ACKNOWLEDGMENTS

This book was made possible by those that support not only the production of this book but also have been supportive of me throughout the years. I am now and forever will be grateful. I want to give a special shoutout to the following individuals that made significant impacts in the creation of the anatomy of financial success. Gloria Bilel and Tanisha Domeaux for being the most supportive throughout the years. Ismeal Carrera, Robin Vahimain and Gricel De Leon for helping in the production of the book. Ron Walter, Crystal Willis, David Hurtado, Donnica Reed, Amanda Tipton, and Sade Taylor for being a vital part of the marketing for this book. I give the most thanks to Gloria Bilel, Tanisha Domeaux, Travis Morgan, Jered Fantroy, and Marketya White for playing a role in both the production and marketing of this book and Neo K Marcellus for being an impactful and guiding writing mentor.

Made in the USA
Las Vegas, NV
14 September 2021